2/19

## Praise for W

"A compact, inspirational pa

—*New York Daily News*

"Readers will appreciate the highly readable, enjoyable, and inspiring true stories along with the book's uplifting message overall." —*Booklist*

"No matter what path readers take, they can gain inspiration here for a life that completes their dreams and uses their abilities." —*Library Journal*

"It's a perfect read to set yourself up for success in 2016."

—BET.com

"The stories pack a punch." —*The Advocate*

"Inspiring . . . After finishing this book, you are likely to listen to your inner voice more and will certainly believe anything is possible." —*Miami Living*

"Moving and motivating." —BroadwayWorld.com

## Praise for *Ten Years Later*

"A thoughtful and inspiring book." —Savannah Guthrie

"It's such a great book. . . . There's a universal quality to these stories." —Kathie Lee Gifford

"I thought the book was fabulous." —Steve Harvey

"The book is filled with these great and wonderful reminders of the capacity of a human being to overcome incredible adversity. . . . A great, great, great reminder of a great country and a great people, and [Hoda] is one of them."

—Mike Huckabee

"Fantastic. It's a great book." —Jimmy Fallon

"I love the book." —Wendy Williams

"Really smart . . . This is a fantastic book . . . a riveting read." —Piers Morgan

"Kotb's book, *Ten Years Later* (written with Jane Lorenzini), offers inspirational profiles of six people who have overcome adversity." —*The New York Times*

"Inspirational." —*USA Today*

"Sobering and inspiring tales in their own right, Kotb's journalistic acumen makes this collection all the more moving."

—*Publishers Weekly*

"Amazing and inspiring stories." —*Ladies' Home Journal*

"Remarkable." —*Access Hollywood*

ALSO BY HODA KOTB

*Hoda: How I Survived War Zones, Bad Hair, Cancer, and Kathie Lee*

*Ten Years Later: Six People Who Faced Adversity and Transformed Their Lives*

# HODA KOTB

## WITH JANE LORENZINI

# WHERE WE BELONG

→→ JOURNEYS ←←

## THAT SHOW US THE WAY

**SIMON & SCHUSTER PAPERBACKS**

NEW YORK  LONDON  TORONTO  SYDNEY  NEW DELHI

Simon & Schuster Paperbacks
An Imprint of Simon & Schuster, Inc.
1230 Avenue of the Americas
New York, NY 10020

First Simon & Schuster trade paperback edition January 2017

SIMON & SCHUSTER PAPERBACKS and colophon are
registered trademarks of Simon & Schuster, Inc.

For information about special discounts for bulk purchases,
please contact Simon & Schuster Special Sales
at 1-866-506-1949 or business@simonandschuster.com.

The Simon & Schuster Speakers Bureau can bring authors to your live event.
For more information or to book an event, contact the
Simon & Schuster Speakers Bureau at 1-866-248-3049
or visit our website at www.simonspeakers.com.

Interior design by Ruth Lee-Mui

Manufactured in the United States of America

3   5   7   9   10   8   6   4   2

The Library of Congress has cataloged the hardcover edition as follows:

Kotb, Hoda, 1964– author.
Where we belong : journeys that show us the way /
Hoda Kotb, with Jane Lorenzini.
pages cm
1. Conduct of life—Case studies. 2. Self-realization—Case studies.
3. Career changes—Case studies. 4. Satisfaction—Case studies.
5. Vocation—Case studies. I. Lorenzini, Jane, author. II. Title.
BJ1589.K67 2016
170'.44—dc23            2015024127

ISBN 978-1-4767-5242-6
ISBN 978-1-4767-5243-3 (pbk)
ISBN 978-1-4767-5244-0 (ebook)

*To Hala, Adel, Jenny, and Jill*

# ✈ CONTENTS ✦

## ✈ INTRODUCTION ✈

Maybe you did it today. You asked yourself: *What the hell am I doing in this job . . . in this relationship . . . in this city?*

Most of us go there. We float around in the half-empty glass, gaze out into the world of possibilities, and wonder:

*Is it too late to do that thing that made me so happy when I was little?*

*Could what matters most to me finally be the center of my life?*

*Can I really trust this yearning voice in my head and long-ing in my heart?*

What we're really asking ourselves . . . from the gut . . . is: *Do I feel like I'm where I belong?*

Lots of us are asking. There are twenty-five times as

many life coaches on duty around the world as there were ten years ago. More and more of us feel it is indeed okay to admit to ourselves—and to someone else—that we feel like we *don't* belong . . . in our careers, our relationships, our overall daily existence. And we're confused about how much control we have in making our lives better, and ideally, the best we can imagine.

Certainly, pinpointing exactly where you belong—where happiness awaits—is tricky.

When you're young, it's difficult to know what will make you happy. When you're older, you finally know what makes you happy, but it's complicated to redirect your many-pronged life. Plus, the head and the heart are such different decision makers. Often, one of the two is a sucker for distractions, excuses, and doubt.

The reaction is interesting when you share with someone the concept of this book. There is a tilt of the head. You can almost hear the mental wheels begin to turn: *Holy cow, I'm not even close to being where I belong in my life right now.* The topic is uncomfortable for some. For others, there is affirmation, a chance to acknowledge that their inner compass is indeed pointed in the right direction. *Well . . . yes. I am where I belong!*

I've known for a long time where I belong, and yet I'm on the slow track to arriving there. I belong with kids, little kids who need guidance and love. Growing up, I thought I'd become a second-grade teacher, but in college, journalism caught my eye and has kept me interested for nearly three decades. I also grew up hoping to one day get married and have three children. That plan, well, had some unexpected snags—divorce, illness, and now, my age. Still, I'll get there . . . to the place where what brings me the most joy brings joy to others, too. I'm thinking a summer camp for underprivileged kids. I can teach them, enjoy their silliness, and hit the pillow knowing I spent the day doing that which has delighted my head and heart for so long.

This book is my way of confirming—maybe even to myself—that it's possible, no matter when, to create a life that's both fun and rewarding. In the pages ahead, you'll meet the extraordinary people who are the proof. These wide-ranging stories offer us all hope that it's never too late, or early, to identify what brings us joy and peace. Some recognize it early in life—as early as grammar school; others need five decades. In this book, you'll experience what it's like for people to realize not only that they're on the wrong path, but also that—yikes!—a leap of faith is the only way to get from Point A to Point Belong.

One story features a young girl who faced a vast chasm between her big dream and the small factory town where she grew up. Burdened by discouraging words and an impoverished upbringing, she worked hard and smart to courageously pursue what she knew she was meant to do. Regret was not an option.

Another story explores the delicate dance of relationship and marriage. When a husband created and followed a fork in the road to pursue personal happiness, his wife felt like their agreed-upon life plan had been knifed in the process. What happened to "us" and "we"? Their journey to feel content as individuals and as a team is compelling.

There is also a story of hope. If you've ever felt that something's missing in your life, but you have no idea what it is, perhaps take a look back over your shoulder. A man in his fifties did and saw something he *never* thought he wanted. That second look changed his world, and now he and his wife work to improve lives around the globe.

You'll also read the story of a woman who, in her thirties, found both love and her place in a community. The unique neighborhood she happened upon in life was rich in ways that the mansion she grew up in could never be. She was finally home.

Tucked in between these intriguing stories will be lovely little offerings from names you know—superstars in their fields. What you may not know is that they too had fish-out-of-water phases in their lives. Before the sparkle of celebrity, there were gray clouds of frustration and worry.

What did it feel like before the road to success revealed itself? How did big fish change directions midstream? Each will identify the guideposts that led to a place of peace and fulfillment.

And so, please read on. These four words will lead the way:

Should.

Would.

Could.

Did.

# WHERE WE BELONG

⇥⤜⇤

If you don't like how things are, change it. You're not a tree. You have the ability to totally transform every area in your life—and it all begins with your very own power of choice.

—JIM ROHN

⇥⤜⇤

# ⇥ MICHELLE HAUSER ⇤

Michelle Hauser started working part-time jobs by the time she turned twelve. She could already tell: no one was going to take care of her better than she could take care of herself.

Instability inserted itself into Michelle's life early. She grew up in Mason City, Iowa, a blue-collar town of twenty-eight thousand people located halfway between Des Moines and Minneapolis, Minnesota. The local hospital was the largest employer, but many of the residents worked in a variety of factories, including Kraft Foods, Armour, and two industrial door manufacturing companies. Michelle's parents, Mike and Laurie, divorced after a nine-year marriage that was challenged by time spent apart.

Mike worked long hours running a struggling diner owned by his alcoholic father. Laurie was a stay-at-home mom until Michelle turned three, when she began working part-time as a radio disc jockey. The couple's relationship suffered under the weight of their busy lives. They divorced in 1988 when Michelle was seven. As agreed upon by the couple, she and her younger brother, James, stayed with Mike during the week so they could remain in the same school district. They spent weekends with Laurie. Both households had drawbacks: Mike was rarely home; Laurie was often at work, with friends, or disabled by untreated depression and anxiety. Michelle found solace playing outdoors. A sensitive child, she was drawn to tending to an injured bug or bird. She was also happy holed up in a quiet room.

"I was chatty if you got me into a conversation," Michelle says, "but otherwise, I was interested in using my imagination out in nature or reading books and drawing. I was a very intellectual kid. I also spent a lot of time in the kitchen experimenting with recipes I found in cookbooks and inside my mom's small metal box filled with handwritten recipe cards."

Mike remarried a year after the divorce and continued to work eighty hours a week at the family restaurant. He took Michelle and James to the restaurant early many mornings and cooked them breakfast, bacon and eggs, before dropping the kids off a block away at grammar school.

"I'd watch him in the kitchen and ask him how to do things," Michelle says of those mornings.

She was too young to be around sharp knives and hot fryers but was allowed to watch how the root beer was made in the basement of the restaurant. At home, Mike taught Michelle basic cooking techniques, even though she couldn't reach the stove.

"I learned how to cook eggs," she describes, "standing on a stool."

In 1991, when Michelle was ten, her grandfather suffered a stroke and the family decided to sell the restaurant. Mike found new work delivering Pepsi products to businesses around town. Long hours continued to keep him away from Michelle and her brother, but the kids were grateful to have a consistent home base. The same couldn't be said about home life with their mother. That year, Michelle's mom gave birth to a baby named Zane. The father was a boyfriend who wanted no part of fatherhood, making Laurie a single mom with three children. Ten-year-old Michelle often cared for James and Zane when her mother went to work or didn't feel well. While Mike worked steadily, Laurie supplemented her inconsistent income with public assistance. She used food stamps at the grocery store and also relied on trips to the local food bank for nonperishables.

"A box of government cheese, cans of peanut butter, containers of corn syrup," Michelle describes. "Food was definitely not a guaranteed thing staying with my mom."

If the pantry ran low, Michelle was not afraid to ask for help, because from time to time, her family had provided for neighbors in need. She remembers at least twice knocking on a door to ask for food.

"I never went hungry because I would go find a way to eat," she says, "but it wouldn't always be *our* food I was eating."

Michelle is not completely clear on why her mother moved in and out of homes frequently, even several times within the same year, other than that it was sometimes for work. Laurie didn't always let the kids know that a move was coming or that it had already happened.

"I kept everything I cared about at my dad's place because sometimes my mom would move when I wasn't around."

Michelle says some of her mother's relatives were involved with illegal drugs. Because the local factory jobs required drug tests, these family members worked as waitresses and shop clerks—or not at all. When one of the relatives watched Michelle and James at her house, Michelle says she sometimes sent them outside to play, locked the door, and used drugs. On other days, the relative used while the kids were inside.

"There would be trays of drugs lying out on the coffee table—methamphetamines or marijuana," Michelle describes. "Sometimes the drugs were put under the couch, but if you dropped a toy on the ground, it would be easy to notice they were there."

Laurie's string of boyfriends brought additional anguish into the kids' daily life. Michelle says one drunk boyfriend held a knife to Michelle's throat as the two watched *Jeopardy!* on television. She was eleven. He was in his thirties.

"He would make me sit there and watch with him. He'd want me to say the answers, but then he would get mad and belligerent if I knew more answers than he did."

The same boyfriend threatened to kill Laurie as he drove drunk with Laurie and Michelle in the car.

"I remember sitting in the backseat with a long metal flashlight—one of those heavy ones—and yelling at him that if he did anything I would beat him in the head with the flashlight. I had to be a survivalist. There were a lot of situations like that."

Michelle couldn't always protect herself. Both parents routinely dropped off Michelle and James at the home of a babysitter who had a son of her own. At age seven, over the course of several months, Michelle was sexually abused by the son, in his twenties.

"I didn't tell anyone for the same reasons many people don't," Michelle explains. "I was embarrassed, ashamed; I was afraid someone would think it was my fault."

While neither parent could know the sitter's house was not safe, Michelle admits that her mother made some poor decisions about who she brought into their lives. She does, however, acknowledge that Laurie was raised by a mother who herself had a number of challenges.

"My mom had a more difficult childhood than I did. So, for her, she was doing a good job."

Despite the chaos and lack of supervision, Michelle was a straight-A student. She didn't need to study to do exceptionally well in school and on standardized tests. Learning was easy and books provided transport to a brighter, more stimulating world.

"I would just sit for hours and hours in my room and read book upon book. In my fifth-grade class we had to have a reading log over the course of the year. You had to read five books . . . I read one hundred and forty."

When Michelle turned eleven, her mom moved to a small town—population eighty-two. Bored and untethered, Michelle and a friend walked eight miles up the railroad tracks to the nearest town, ate lunch, and walked back home.

"No one really kept track of me when I was little," she says. "Even during my teens I had free rein. When I was sixteen I didn't see my dad for nearly two weeks because our schedules didn't align."

By age twelve, Michelle had her first job. She worked alongside migrant workers picking strawberries.

"I don't know how older people do it," Michelle says, "because I remember having achy knees as a kid."

She wanted to earn her own money; she needed to. "I knew I couldn't depend on anyone else to do that for me, so I wanted to make sure I could if I had to."

At fourteen, with a work permit, Michelle landed a job at a restaurant waitressing, filling the salad bar, and washing dishes. By law she was too young to work with heat or knives, but some of the managers ignored the rules and assigned her to the grill. Within a year, Michelle began to get caught up in the wrong crowd at the restaurant. Most of her coworkers were older and some used drugs openly and offered them to staff members while on the job. She began to sample pot, cocaine, meth, PCP, psychedelic mushrooms, LSD, and heroin.

"I hadn't had a close-knit family structure or people I felt cared about me, so these were some of the first people who were accepting of me," she says. "Looking back, I hung out with them because I felt like I belonged. It would be ten or eleven o'clock at night when I got off work and no one was regularly checking to see that I came home."

Michelle's drug use turned out to be a plus at school. It established a common bond with classmates who also used, which resulted in new "friendships."

"They suddenly had an interest in talking to me and hanging out with me."

Even with drugs in her life, Michelle continued to excel in school. She was working nearly a combined forty hours a week at the restaurant and also as a bill collector over the phone. Yet, although barely cracking a book, she maintained solid As. While Michelle's daily life revolved around work and drugs, she believed her brainpower would eventually launch her out of Mason City and into a more intellectual environment.

"My main goal when I was younger was to not end up as an unskilled worker like my family members."

Michelle's secret dream was to become a doctor. A nurturer at heart, she loved the idea of caring for and curing people for a living.

"People would say, 'Oh, you always seem to want to make everybody and everything feel better. You would make a good doctor.' That kind of stuck with me."

But how? Without role models, finances, or connec-
tions, how could a girl from a small town in Iowa whose
daily life revolved around an unsavory crowd and double-
shift work hours realize her ambitious dream?

"Every handful of years, someone would make the
comment about how I was really smart, and those few
comments were really what got me through," she says. "If I
didn't have that subjective data, there was nothing else telling me I was going to be able to be a doctor."

Nothing else and no one else. In her junior year of high
school, Michelle had a meeting with her guidance counselor.

"When I walked into this woman's office she said,
'What do you want to do when you grow up?' and I said,
'I want to be a doctor.' She actually laughed under her
breath and said, 'Let's find something more suitable for
you to do.'"

Even after the counselor looked through Michelle's file
and saw how academically gifted she was, she still advised,
"I think what would be a great job for you would be to go
work in a factory."

But, by age sixteen, Michelle was determined more
than ever to take control of her destiny by working hard
and staying self-reliant. Still partying with friends, Michelle had two jobs and was paying for essentials like

shampoo and clothes. She also bought a car and car insurance. Michelle told her father she wanted to move out on her own. Concerned about his daughter's drug use—he knew only about the pot—Mike tried to set ground rules, which didn't go over well.

"I felt like, I buy all my own stuff, I make my own money for future rent. You can't just decide you're going to make a bunch of rules for me now when I've never had any, especially when you're not doing the things for me that most parents do."

At seventeen, after she completed her high school requirements, Michelle began dating a man named Josh, whom she met at a party. He was twenty years old and they indulged in drugs together. Looking back now, Michelle understands why his "I love you" drew her to him.

"I thought he was a rare catch. Here was someone who cared about me. I didn't realize it was very normal, that it's what people *should* have in their life."

Both quickly decided to stop using drugs and alcohol; they'd had enough. The pair was engaged in 1998 and Michelle agreed to join Josh at the Assembly of God church services he attended. By then, Michelle's father had developed a small real estate business and offered them an apartment at fair market rates, which they accepted.

The next decision was one seventeen-year-old Michelle

loathed making, but she couldn't ignore the need for health benefits and a steady income. The cafeteria job she had at the local community college had ended, so she started work at a door factory located in town. Still, she didn't lose sight of her dream to one day enroll in medical school and become a doctor.

"College was always in the plan, but, depending on the day," she says with a soft laugh, "it seemed less or more feasible."

Michelle was proficient at math, so factory managers assigned her the task of applying accurate measurements on each door to indicate where the hinges should be attached. She and another worker measured and marked, and the door moved on. Because measurements were required on both sides, a machine was used to flip over the door. Just a few months into the job, the machine broke on a day when Michelle and a female coworker were measuring an extremely heavy hospital door with a lead core.

"A supervisor yelled at me and another woman, demanding that we flip the door over by hand or he'd find other workers who would. I needed the job and I'd just gotten hired, and they told me that if I was ever late or did anything wrong I'd be fired, no questions asked. So, I tried my best to flip the door over."

Something popped in Michelle's back. So excruciating

was the pain that she couldn't move her arms. Michelle
was transported to the emergency room for an X ray. She'd
not broken any bones but suffered soft tissue damage. A
general physician prescribed pain medication and recommended work restrictions regarding limited standing and
lifting. Michelle immediately returned to work on an overnight shift but was unable to perform her duties. Within
two weeks, weary of being called "worthless" and cursed at
by a factory manager, Michelle quit.

Josh and Michelle were married that June in his parents' backyard. His grandmother made Michelle's dress
and her father catered the low-key party afterward; their
religion disallowed dancing and drinking.

In August 1999, following months of therapy on her
back, neck, and arms, Michelle decided to honor her aspirations and go to college. She chose a Christ-centered
Pentecostal school because of her immersion in Josh's strict
religion. Bolstered by academic scholarships and financial
aid, Michelle enrolled in North Central University in Minneapolis, two hours north of Mason City. She decided to
major in psychology (a way to treat people without requir-
ing a medical degree) and biblical studies. The couple lived
in a one-bedroom apartment in downtown Minneapolis
and both found work delivering pizzas. Always interested
in cooking with her father and baking with her mother,

Michelle also took a job in a gourmet deli located inside a high-end grocery store in the city. She was exposed for the first time to imported food and flavors from around the world. Michelle took a third job working as a chef's assistant and inventory clerk at a local cooking store.

At eighteen, she had begun her journey toward higher education and even higher expectations for her future. Her mother was on board with Michelle's decision, though distracted by a crumbling second marriage and subsequent divorce she was dealing with in Florida. Michelle's father and stepmother, Rose, were silently skeptical about both the rigid religion and the Bible college.

"I'd gotten married very young to someone I hadn't known for very long. I had gone from being a very good kid most of my childhood to having a few rocky years in high school, even though I still got good grades. Then I got involved in a new religion that was way out there. But they knew that if they said that they didn't want me to do something, I would do it."

By May 2000, two semesters later, even Michelle thought the religion-centered college was a bad idea. Put off by what she perceived as the school's exclusionary views and severe doctrines, she left North Central.

"I thought, *Well, maybe everyone was right. I'm just not cut out for college.*"

She also left the Assembly of God church, opting instead to worship at a Baptist church.

Determined to continue educating herself, Michelle enrolled fifteen minutes away at Le Cordon Bleu College of Culinary Arts. She would complete an accelerated fourteen-month program that offered training in classical cooking methods, the art of French pastry, and professional baking. Michelle already felt comfortable in the kitchen and deduced that learning a sophisticated trade was at least a step up from remaining an unskilled worker. But, once again, Mike was not keen on Michelle's plan.

"This was the worst for him. He'd been a cook and he knew that he'd slaved away eighty hours a week and he barely got by. He was hoping that I would do better for myself."

With few opportunities for scholarships to Le Cordon Bleu, Michelle knew she'd have to work forty hours a week and also procure loans to cover the $25,000 tuition.

"The thing that has always kept my credit good is that one time my dad told me, 'If I don't give you any other advice, pay your bills on time.'" She laughs. "Even though I was raised with zero financial planning information, there were a few things like that which really stuck with me, and that's been super helpful."

Classes started in September 2000, and within weeks Michelle knew she'd made the right decision.

"I really enjoyed it. I was excited to go every day, and there wasn't a whole lot that had happened before this program that I was excited about."

Michelle had gone through a rebellion-based vegetarian phase in high school and remained a non-meat-eater thereafter for ethical and health reasons. She did, however, sample every kind of food in cooking school. She excelled at the academics and the hands-on work. With a laugh she describes a day when the butchery teacher instructed the class to break down large pieces of meat into restaurant-sized servings.

"He was completely irate because people weren't doing a very good job. He yelled, 'The goddamn vegetarian chef is doing the best work!'"

Halfway through the Le Cordon Bleu program, despite her success and enjoyment, twenty-year-old Michelle felt a distracting urge to look beyond the kitchen. Her real dream was tapping on the shoulder of her chef's coat.

"I started to realize that if I was at the end of my life and looked back, I would really regret not trying to go to medical school. So, at that point I thought, *It doesn't really matter to me if I fail, but I would regret not trying.*"

Josh backed Michelle's idea to pursue medical school and a two-pronged plan was formed. Because the Le Cordon Bleu program required students to land a four-week internship anywhere in the world, Michelle searched for a restaurant that was also close to an affordable college with a premed program. She found the perfect pairing in California: Chez Panisse in Berkeley and, 280 miles north, Humboldt State University in Arcata. She would start classes at Humboldt once she finished her four-week cooking internship. Le Cordon Bleu would allow her to receive her *diplôme* through the mail and not have to fly home to Minnesota to graduate from the program.

Together now for nearly four years, Michelle and Josh were both excited about an adventure out west. In late August 2001, they drove their belongings from Minneapolis to Arcata and moved into a double-wide trailer with Josh's brother and his brother's friend, who were also enrolled in Humboldt. They then drove south to Berkeley so Michelle could do her internship at Chez Panisse (ranked that year by *Gourmet* magazine as the "Best Restaurant in the United States") from October to November 2001. Though Josh had promised to get a job in Berkeley, Michelle says he instead met up with friends each day to skateboard. She focused on training at the award-winning restaurant.

Michelle was instantly captivated by the fresh approach to food and cooking at Chez Panisse. Chefs created daily menus that featured local, sustainably sourced, organic, seasonal ingredients.

"It was, hands down, the most delicious food I'd eaten in my whole life. I'd never had vegetables and fruit that tasted so good. That really inspired me to learn the techniques that allow you to create flavorful, healthful food."

Michelle wanted to learn, literally, from the ground up. She asked her supervisors for permission to leave the kitchen for a few days so she could spend time at the main farm that supplied the restaurant and nearby farmers' markets.

"It was so different from what I had seen in Iowa, with the monoculture and cornfields and hog farms. Here was a hippie farmer with a long beard and his field had a lot of weeds in it, which was not acceptable in my dad's garden or in the fields in Iowa. We'd walk through the garden and this farmer would say, 'Here are the carrots,' and I'd think, *I don't see the carrots.* But he dug under a bunch of weeds and said, 'The sun is so hot it would scorch everything, so this is how I keep from having to water so much.'" Michelle was fascinated. "I found all of it very eye opening. It made me realize that you shouldn't assume things have to be done one certain way. There might be somebody out there doing it in a completely different way. It opened my mind up about a lot of things, not just food."

By November 2001, twenty-year-old Michelle had completed the internship and secured her *diplôme* from

Prepping at Chez Panisse, Berkeley, 2001 *(Courtesy of Michelle Hauser)*

Le Cordon Bleu. Months later, in January 2002, Michelle would begin tackling the premed program at Humboldt State in Arcata. Once more, a combination of academic scholarships, financial aid, and working forty hours a week would make Michelle's college experience possible. Mike—again—was nervous for his daughter and what he saw as unnecessary crushing debt.

"My family, especially my dad, grew up with the philosophy that you don't take out loans for things that you can't pay back. He didn't think it made sense financially at all."

Michelle says she never perceived the financial challenge as a mountain; her daily life had always been riddled with perpetual molehills that she addressed one day at a time.

"I think I lived in survival mode most of the time, always thinking, *How am I going to pay the bills this month?* That almost shielded me somewhat from thinking it would all be too overwhelming, because I was always focused on what needed to be done right now."

She was also a confident workhorse with newly acquired horsepower. While Josh once again delivered pizzas, Michelle's *diplôme* allowed her to land higher-paying jobs in the food industry. She found work as a consultant and pastry chef at an all-organic vegetarian restaurant. She

was also hired as cooking school manager at a retail cook-
ware store called Pacific Flavors. As an added service to its
customers, the store brought in local chefs to teach home
cooks various preparation techniques and menu planning.
Part of Michelle's job was to develop course content, but
the owner made sure to declare one category off-limits.

"She told me, 'The one thing you cannot do is have
healthy-cooking classes because no one likes them and no
one will sign up for them.'"

Michelle's most important job of all was getting familiar with the premed program at Humboldt. Her major
was cellular/molecular biology and she was assigned a premed adviser. Michelle was thankful for any guidance on
what she needed to do to graduate and to get accepted at a
medical school. Jacob Varkey, a biology professor and PhD,
outlined for Michelle a road map to success.

"He told me I needed to get all As," she says, "especially coming from a small high school in the middle of
nowhere."

Jacob also identified the score Michelle needed to
make on the Medical College Admission Test (MCAT)
and advised her to create a structured study plan to
achieve it. He told her that laboratory research should
be a component of her résumé, along with extracurricular
activities. He suggested volunteer work at an area hospital

to help Michelle get a general feel for a career in medicine. Jacob also recommended listing her extensive past and current employment hours on the résumé to illustrate to admissions committees her work ethic, her financial challenges, and the reason why she was attending a lesser-known university.

"Michelle impressed me most with her persistence. She made a point to come and see me every semester and even sometimes once or twice during the semester," Jacob explains, "which is very rare for students to do because they get busy with their coursework and other activities. But Michelle was very consistent. During the appointment she would tell me what she was doing, and then she'd want to know what else she should be doing, what's the next step."

Clearly, Michelle had the drive and the smarts to manage the academic workload, but in spring 2002 she would find out just how gifted a mind she was given.

"It was on a dare," she says with a laugh.

One evening, Michelle was ribbing Josh for rarely making dinner. Knowing how smart Michelle was, he promised to cook if she would take the Mensa exam, a test given to identify people with extremely high IQs. Mensa members are those who score at or better than 98 percent of the general population. Michelle accepted the dare and took the test at the College of the Redwoods in nearby Eureka. She wasn't sure if she would pass. The format was very different from a standardized test; questions involved logic and deductive reasoning. But when the results arrived, Josh cooked dinner and Michelle added *Member of Mensa, United States*, to her résumé.

In fall 2002, Michelle was extremely busy, studying for first-semester finals at Humboldt and working thirty hours a week. After nearly four years together, Josh and Michelle were crafting very different lives in terms of education and career paths. One night, after a full day of school and work, Michelle received an ultimatum from Josh.

"He said that even though we agreed that I'd go to college, he decided he wanted a wife who would stay home and take care of kids. He said, 'If you don't want to do that then we can't stay married.'"

Having known for years that their aspirations in life were very different, Michelle moved out. She took the couple's old pickup and for nearly a week, slept in the truck, showered in the university's gym, took finals, and went to work. She then found a trailer to rent with a roommate.

The new semester and year would bring exciting opportunities for Michelle. In summer 2003, she began to explore the world on a molecular level in the laboratory. The American Heart Association awarded her a scholarship to conduct cardiovascular and bioengineering research at the University of California, San Diego. With little money to spare, she stayed with various friends in Southern California and slept on their couches. When she wasn't working in the lab, Michelle enjoyed walking on the beach to clear her head and sort through the final details of her divorce. She even began to jog. Over the course of one summer, regular exercise and the healthy cooking techniques she learned at Chez Panisse proved to be a powerful combination.

"I realized I felt so much better. I'd never been a physically active person before. I lost quite a bit of weight and felt better about myself."

The professor who oversaw the laboratory at UCSD where Michelle was doing summer research work was so pleased with her performance that he invited her to stay. She politely declined, explaining that her focus was on completing her premed coursework and applying to med school. The girl from Iowa with the strong work ethic, consistently high grades, and can-do attitude was proving herself to others and to Jacob.

"He got really excited for me and basically said, 'You're doing great. Don't screw anything up and you should get into a medical school somewhere,'" she says, laughing. "He became a cheerleader for me."

Over the next two years, Michelle immersed herself in

premed courses and lab research at Humboldt. She continued to rely on guidance from Jacob, and also from married biology professors Patty Siering and Mark Wilson, who directed her toward impactful genetics and microbiology research projects to add to her résumé. At work, she began to consider incorporating her newfound passion for healthy living into classes at Pacific Flavors.

In her own life, Michelle had discovered that a vegan diet solved her problem with dairy allergies and also her past struggles with weight. Surely many other people could benefit from good-tasting food that also accommodated their medical conditions or desire to feel better. Although she had been advised not to offer healthy-cooking classes, Michelle knew her students were curious about the topic.

"People would ask, 'How can I make that with less sugar?' or 'My family member has diabetes. Can they eat this?'"

Michelle turned to the Internet to better educate herself on the effects of food on the body. She utilized PubMed, a free online database that accesses studies in the US National Library of Medicine. With the information she gathered and her own story of success, Michelle convinced her boss to let her teach a course on how to prepare good-tasting healthy food. Michelle's instincts were right; the class consistently sold out.

Education was her next focus. Michelle went to Jacob and told him she was interested in exposing low-income kids—whose parents may not have gone to college—to the concept of higher education. Jacob supported the idea and was already looking into developing an educational program at Humboldt for underserved kids. Online, Michelle found a similar program based at Stanford University and offered her help to the organizers. In early 2005, through Stanford, Michelle served as a teacher and mentor to minority and low-income high school students on an Indian reservation in Covelo, California. She shared with students how to effectively navigate a path to college. She also showed kids how to properly fill out paperwork for scholarships and financial aid.

Now twenty-four years old, nearly four years after she moved to California to pursue her dream, it was time for Michelle to do some navigating of her own. She needed to register to take the MCAT and determine which medical schools she wanted to target. Michelle would have to be choosy; the application process was expensive and airfare to interview destinations would be as well. She'd need to fly first out of the small Arcata/Eureka Airport to connect with flights departing from large airports like San Francisco International.

After passing the MCAT, Michelle was preparing her applications to send to med schools. She had no idea that eighteen hundred miles east, serendipity was cozied up next to her father at a picnic table in Audubon, Iowa.

At a family reunion, Michelle's father, Mike, was sitting across the table from his cousin Nordahl and Nordahl's wife, Suzanne, whom Mike had never met. He mentioned to the couple that Michelle was preparing to apply to medical schools. Nordahl and Suzanne excitedly revealed that she worked as director of the premedical advising program at the University of Vermont. Suzanne gave Mike her e-mail and phone number to pass along to his daughter.

In the months ahead, Michelle and Suzanne corresponded about the application process. When Suzanne reviewed Michelle's curriculum vitae and grades, she offered an idea.

"She said, 'You know, they really like quirky people at Harvard. You should apply to Harvard.' I thought, *I am not wasting two hundred dollars applying to Harvard.*" Michelle laughs and adds, "*They do not want me at Harvard.*"

Not only did Michelle think she had no shot at Harvard, she didn't want to live on the East Coast.

In September 2005, Michelle sent applications to twelve different medical schools; Harvard was not on the list. For financial reasons, she chose to interview with just three of the schools that offered invitations: the University of Iowa, the University of California at San Francisco, and the University of California at San Diego. Persistent, Suzanne continued to encourage Michelle to apply to Harvard before the October application deadline. Her confidence was rooted in the unique breadth of Michelle's life experiences: she had worked on farms, taught in cooking schools, volunteered on a Native American reservation, and excelled in cardiovascular bioengineering and genetics research.

"Suzanne said that Harvard likes people who aren't the perfect cookie-cutter type," Michelle explains.

Ultimately, Michelle decided to honor Suzanne's suggestion and apply to Harvard. She then flew to interviews in November and December at UCSD, U of I, and UCSF, all of which offered her enrollment in their medical schools. She had declined all other interview offers that came her way due to the expense and because she preferred to stay in California.

One school never responded: Harvard. Michelle was not surprised. She accepted the offer at UCSF.

In late December 2005, Michelle flew home to Iowa to visit family for several weeks. One afternoon in early January, she decided to study at a coffee shop while her father and stepmom worked. Scanning through her e-mails, Michelle noticed an entry in her spam folder. She clicked it open, anticipating a quick delete. Not so fast. The contents stunned and alarmed her.

"The Harvard invitation request went to my spam e-mail! I about had a heart attack," she says, laughing. "One: I just couldn't believe it, and two: I thought, *Of all the times something goes to my spam folder, why this?!*"

And even worse, she says, "I didn't notice it until after my interview date had passed."

Michelle immediately contacted administrators at Harvard and was relieved by their accommodating attitude.

"They said, 'We have one interview day left, so if you can make it out here, you can interview.'"

Michelle flew from Iowa back to California to get the one interview suit she owned. She then boarded another plane and flew to Boston, her first-ever trip to the East Coast. Michelle made sure to share the news about the Harvard interview with Suzanne, Jacob, and the professors who had supported her throughout her three years at Humboldt. They were overjoyed. She describes her father's reaction to the prestigious opportunity as "speaking Iowan."

"You don't ever tell people things that would give them a big head; you don't brag about yourself. That's just how you are in Iowa when you're there," she explains. "So, he said something briefly, like, 'That's exciting,' but he was pretty low-key about it."

Mike may have been reserved with Michelle, but she

heard from friends in Mason City that he was amazed and full of pride.

"It meant a lot. I didn't grow up with people hugging me or saying 'I love you.' I would bring home straight As and no one would say a word. I was rarely told anything positive about myself, so to hear that he was proud of me really meant a lot. I think that was the point in time he realized that I *did* know what I was doing," she says, and laughs.

The morning of Michelle's interview, she and a group of candidates gathered for a presentation about the benefits of attending Harvard Medical School. They sat together in the stately, multi-pillared Gordon Hall on the campus of the medical school.

"You can imagine how imposing this looked," she recalls, "to someone of my background."

The interviewees were told they had been selected from the as many as 7,000 applications the medical school receives each year. Only 165 of the approximately 1,000 interviewed that year would become the class of 2010. Michelle then split from the large group and began individual interviews with a current student and faculty members.

"I was definitely very anxious and awed—kind of in shock that I was there."

As the day moved forward, Michelle felt more at ease;

everyone was kind and the conversations flowed well. By two o'clock, she was finished and headed to the airport for a cross-country flight home. Michelle called her father and Rose, and her mother.

"I told them I felt really confident about the interviews and thought I might get in. I *never* say anything like that or feel that confident about anything. I'm not sure what it was, but I just had a feeling."

Because Arcata, the small town where Michelle was attending Humboldt, has no nearby interstate and only a small airport, mail arrives late and sometimes out of order.

"My financial aid letter from Harvard arrived before my acceptance letter," she says, chuckling. "I thought, *I guess this means I got in.*"

The acceptance letter arrived a few days later.

"I was totally over the moon. I just could not believe I got into Harvard Medical School."

Michelle shared the amazing letter with her parents, her supporters at Humboldt, and Suzanne.

"I had that *Wow* reaction," Suzanne recalls. "Still, I wasn't that surprised. She was on a roll, getting quick acceptances at some of the best medical schools in the country. I joked with her, 'Nice problem you have, Michelle.'"

Harvard truly was an incredible opportunity, but Michelle was torn. UCSF or Harvard? She listed pros and cons for both. Michelle loved living in California but was interested in the opportunity to explore the East Coast. She also understood the impact the word "Harvard" had on a résumé.

"I felt like the name recognition might help me pool resources to work on the projects I wanted to work on to help underserved folks in a variety of ways that I might not get going to UC San Francisco," she explains, "which may or may not be true, but at the time, that's what I thought."

On the final day to decline or accept, Michelle chose Harvard. But before the next exciting chapter of her life could begin, Michelle had to close the last, dressed in a cap and gown. In May 2006, she graduated from Humboldt State summa cum laude with a bachelor of science in cellular/molecular biology and a minor in chemistry. Now twenty-five years old, Michelle packed a trailer with her belongings and drove with a friend from California to Boston, home to the campus of Harvard Medical School. Financial aid and need-based scholarships covered tuition and a small slice of the high cost of living in Boston. But, because of the academic workload, Michelle would not be able to hold down several jobs as she had in the past. The additional money Michelle needed for bills, food, and books came from her father and stepmother. They'd been giving her $500 per month since 2005 to help reduce the stress of her busy work and school schedule.

"It was a big sacrifice for them because they've never had a lucrative income. The way they could swing it was by spending very little on themselves, never really traveling or taking vacations, living in a modest house in a very inexpensive, small Iowa town, and not having any loans," she says. "They don't expect me to pay them back, but eventually, I will."

In August 2006, Michelle began her adventure in medical school. Her plan was not only to get a medical degree but also to identify an area of medicine that she could improve.

"I knew that eighty percent of diseases in the US are based on lifestyle, so surely that area was already being addressed as a component of the medical school curriculum," she says. "But when I got to Harvard, I realized, *Actually, very few people are focusing on this angle; there is a big gap to step into.*"

Within months at school, Michelle crossed paths with a man who shared her interest in the link between good health and lifestyle. At an alternative medicine forum she attended, Michelle met David Eisenberg, an associate professor of medicine at Harvard who was hosting the event. He asked each of the attendees to share something about him- or herself.

"I said, 'I used to be a chef and I'm interested in

combining nutrition and medicine,'" Michelle recalls. "He said to me, 'This has nothing to do with what we're discussing here, but I really want to talk to you about that, so make an appointment with my secretary and come talk to me about it.'"

Dr. Eisenberg had the idea of working with the Culinary Institute of America to develop a conference that would teach physicians, registered dieticians, and other healthcare professionals about the combined power of nutrition and good-tasting food. Michelle was not only excited about the project, she was also eager to pinpoint effective ways to motivate people to make healthy lifestyle changes. After extensive planning, a first-of-its-kind conference was held at the CIA at Greystone in St. Helena, California: "Healthy Kitchens, Healthy Lives: Caring for Our Patients and Ourselves." Michelle was thrilled to be involved with the program as a co-lecturer and culinary educator. But while David's dream was to educate professionals about nutrition and good health, Michelle was eager to bring the message of prevention to patients, especially in underserved communities.

"When I was a kid, after school, I would let myself into the house and make two microwave burritos with cheese on them and sour cream on top of that for a snack," Michelle recalls. "I just didn't know anything about healthy eating at all. It wasn't something that my parents talked to

me about or tried to change. They just didn't know; they
didn't understand what was going on."

Ironically, though, medical school was not going to be
an easy place to promote prevention. Michelle was shocked
to learn that within her four years of curriculum, a mere
4.5 hours of lecture time would be devoted to nutrition,
and even then, the material was limited to learning how
to recognize vitamin deficiencies and several other basic
principles. She also observed during rounds with attending physicians that patients were not being taught that a
healthy lifestyle is a key component of disease prevention.
When she made the effort to speak with patients about the
importance of diet and exercise, some attending physicians
discouraged her approach.

"It would almost be a slap on the wrist," she says. "They
would talk down about it and say, 'It's not worth wasting
your time; no one's going to make any changes.'"

But Michelle silently disagreed, recalling the student
success stories at the Pacific Flavors cooking school.

"I thought, *I've seen people make changes and not have to
be on insulin anymore or on blood pressure medicine. I've seen
them lower their cholesterol and stop their antidepressant medi-
cations.* Clearly these doctors had not seen that."

The restrictive environment was isolating for Michelle.

"It made me feel like I didn't fit in," she says. "It's

frowned upon in med school to do something different from what an authority figure tells you, so I felt like I had to hide who I was and not talk about the things I liked. I had to go through the motions to get through a short rotation so I could get decent grades and eventually go do the things I wanted to do."

In August 2007, at the start of her second year of medical school, Michelle took the one nutrition course offered. Eager to further explore the topic, she approached the course director about getting more involved with the class and nutrition-related projects. The director listened. Soon after, Michelle was invited to join a committee that linked Harvard's schools of medicine and public health. Members were tasked with finding ways to increase the nutrition education curriculum for medical students.

"The main theme of med school is not prevention, it's treatment," she says. "But you find your group of people and then you feel more comfortable, and you become very close with those people because you realize you're on the outside."

In 2009, at twenty-eight years old, Michelle elected to stay an extra year in school to get a master's degree in public policy and administration from Harvard's Kennedy School of Government. She felt an MPA would help her understand how to best navigate the politics and social aspects of making change for the better—whatever she determined that to be—on a large scale.

"I realized that to actually make changes that the entire public sees and not just that you do individually in an office with one patient, there would have to be some sort of policy change. A lot of the reasons I wasn't healthy when I was growing up had to do with lack of education and lack of access to things that make you healthy, like walking trails and fresh fruits and vegetables prepared in delicious ways. I needed to understand politics, how to make policy, and how to inspire people to bring about those changes."

The burden of funding yet another degree was lifted when she landed the highly competitive Zuckerman Fellowship. The award fully funded her MPA and also provided a $30,000 stipend, money that relieved the financial strain on Michelle's dad and the guilt she felt for borrowing from him. As a Zuckerman Fellow, Michelle spent the next year attending weekly meetings with a diverse range of professionals discussing effective ways to make positive changes in the world.

"We sat around with all these powerful and influential people and they were saying to us, 'You guys are the ones who need to figure out solutions to really big, well-known problems,'" she explains. "There's really a burden on me and all the people who've been given these gifts and opportunities to try to fix things and make things better in the world."

The MPA studies exposed Michelle to a network of students from seventy-two different countries, a potentially critical component to broadly integrate whatever positive solution she may develop one day.

"It made my world bigger and allowed me to interact with people I never would have had the chance to," she says. "Now I can always find someone to reach out to for an answer to a question or to make a connection."

The same year, in July 2009, Michelle built her own website focused on healthy eating. With one foot in medical school, she wanted to plant the other firmly in nutrition. The cyber world seemed lacking in reliable sources on the topic of healthy eating, and Michelle felt she could credibly put the power of prevention in the hands of visitors to her site. She also loved the idea of interacting with people—this time through videos and postings—as she'd done during cooking classes at Pacific Flavors.

Several months into her final year of medical school, Michelle began submitting applications to residency programs around the country through the online Electronic Residency Application Service (ERAS). She decided to specialize in internal medicine, which deals with the prevention, diagnosis, and treatment of adult diseases.

"It's harder when we're older to change our habits, so that's why I decided to work with adults instead of kids. I feel like there's a big hole there in working with adults on these sorts of things."

By early 2011, she had already undergone several interviews with residency programs she liked, including her first choice, Cambridge Health Alliance at Harvard Medical School. Michelle wanted to continue her work with underserved patients in CHA's community clinic system. CHA also allowed for regular rotations in hospitals outside the alliance, which interested Michelle.

The next step required the ERAS system to implement a "best fit" algorithm and match applicants with a residency program.

"Right around March fifteenth," Michelle explains, "you go to your medical school and there's a big pile of envelopes waiting. At noon on that day, everyone across the country opens their envelopes and finds out at the very same time where they got into residency."

Good news was tucked inside Michelle's envelope. She was matched with Cambridge, her first choice.

One month later, an even more significant match was made, this time in Michelle's personal life. Over the past year, she had been on dozens of failed dates with men she'd met through an online dating service. Strapped for time and discouraged by the results, she logged into her account in April so she could cancel her subscription.

"I had gone on between fifty to sixty dates and I didn't hit it off with anyone," she says. "But then I saw this picture and thought, *Oh, he's cute. Maybe I'll look at his profile real quick.*"

The site had saved the best for last—she met Jason Wimmert, who'd recently moved to Boston and worked for Procter & Gamble. Michelle learned that during college, Jason played soccer and built homes in other countries through Habitat for Humanity. Like Michelle, he enjoyed the outdoors, running, and traveling. The two began dating. Within three months, they moved in together.

In May 2011, Michelle achieved her childhood dream and then some. Thirty-year-old Michelle graduated in less than five years with both an MD and an MPA from Harvard Medical School and the Kennedy School of Government, respectively.

Two months later, Michelle Hauser, MD, MPA, began a three-year residency program that included two significant changes: she would receive a paycheck (about $50,000 to start), and she used the word "doctor" when introducing herself to patients.

Throughout medical school and her residency, Michelle worked and trained in four area hospitals and several

Graduation from Harvard Medical School and the Kennedy School of Government, Boston, 2011 *(Courtesy of Commencement Photos, Inc.)*

community clinics. She rotated through a variety of specialties and was drawn to treating patients from underserved communities in clinical settings.

"I knew they must be thinking, *What does this white, blond woman from Harvard know about being a poor immigrant from another country?* But a lot of them worked in a factory or in a field or had to figure out how to get by, so I often found something that we had in common, even through an interpreter, and that put them at ease. I think that being a doctor is more than just knowing medicine. It's also about making people feel comfortable and confident that you have their best interest in mind."

By the end of the first year of residency, Michelle began to adapt to the rapid pace of the program, the sleep deprivation, and the pressure of working eighty hours a week.

"I used to have to study where it was really quiet with no distractions, and now I can study next to a jackhammer," she says, laughing.

In the minimal hours she spent at home, Michelle valued Jason's consistently caring attitude and calm temperament.

"He's a solid, dependable, bright partner. He's also more fun and lighthearted than I am and never gets stressed. That's exactly what I needed and still do!"

Michelle was thirty-one when she entered her second year of residency. Her role changed dramatically. Instead of participating in rotations as an intern with attending physicians approving her every decision, Michelle was now in charge of teaching and managing a team of interns and medical students.

By 2013/2014, her final year of residency, Michelle was focused on trusting her instincts—*How sick are patients? What care do they need?* The years of intense training were structured to ultimately produce a confident, competent physician who was ready to self-manage her career.

"Someone may barely check in with you during the day, because within a few months you're going to be on your own as an attending physician yourself," she explains, "so you need to be able to do the work."

In the final few months of the program, Michelle worked the overnight shift. Only one attending doctor in the entire hospital was available if she needed help—if there was time to ask. One night, a patient on the floor developed a hole in her lung. Michelle made calls to the attending and the cardiothoracic surgeon, but there was no time to wait. She needed to immediately, on her own, stick a needle in the patient's chest to release air that was compressing the lung and heart and interfering with the organs' abilities to function properly.

"I had seen videos and done it on dummies, but never on a live patient," Michelle says, "but I knew I was able to do it and I did. Luckily, the cardiothoracic surgeon arrived a few minutes later to take over."

On balance, Michelle found the residency experience both extremely exciting and incredibly taxing. Life for three years was restricted to learning and training.

"You can't be the type of family member, friend, or partner you wish you could be. You work long hours, the pager is always beeping, you miss holidays, you're sleep deprived," she says. "You always feel like you're failing at interpersonal relationships during residency."

On June 30, 2014, Michelle graduated from the internal medicine residency program at Cambridge Health Alliance at Harvard. The thirty-three-year-old was now free to focus on a very important personal project: her wedding. Michelle and Jason were getting married on July 12 and had less than two weeks to drive across the country from Boston to Northern California's wine country.

The couple exchanged vows surrounded by friends, family, and lush vineyards. The honeymoon, eight hours north in Oregon, was a mix of relaxation and work; Michelle had to study for the internal medicine board exam in August.

In September 2014, Michelle had one last academic

Michelle and Jason, Northern California,
2014 *(Courtesy of James Hall, Bustle & Twine)*

challenge. She started a three-year postdoctoral research fellowship in cardiovascular disease prevention and a master's degree program in epidemiology at Stanford University. She and Jason had moved back to California so she could continue her schooling. Still with Procter & Gamble, Jason works as a program manager, overseeing the manufacturing quality-control processes domestically and around the globe. He travels frequently and is able to maintain a location-free role with the company.

The three-year program at Stanford is custom-designed and fully funded for Michelle, comprised of a three-year research stipend and a two-year master of science degree in epidemiology. Before she graduates in May 2017, Michelle will spend her days treating patients in a primary care clinic, conducting research focused on prevention for Stanford via a grant from the National Institutes of Health, and learning how to write funding grants. She will earn approximately $50,000 per year. Throughout, Michelle will be on the lookout for a large-scale problem that needs a creative solution.

"I feel like there's something out there that I'm meant to do, and I don't feel like I've gotten to that exact thing yet; it's in the realm of food and nutrition and policy making. It might sound silly, but that's a huge stress for me. I feel like I've been given a lot of gifts and opportunities along the way, so I'm always asking myself, *Am I supposed to be doing more? Is there something different I should be doing?*"

Michelle does know that it will be a combination of professional challenges that will keep her brain stimulated and her heart satisfied. She'd like to structure her work life with a mix of research, teaching, treating patients, improving her website focused on healthy living (ChefinResidency .com), and affecting positive policy change.

"I've been on rotations where someone comes to you with a problem and you stitch it up or cut it out or give them medicine and it goes away; it's a lot of instant gratification. I'm happy doing those things, but I'm overwhelmed by a nagging feeling that I have to do something that's going to get to the root of, and prevent, the problem. My focus will be on people eating better and being more active, and trying to figure out ways to do that on a community level and identifying the reasons that are preventing people from doing both."

Michelle describes her college debt—$90,000—as minimal compared to most med school graduates', not only because she was diligent about filling out financial aid and scholarship forms, but also due to her extremely underprivileged background. She knew, too, that Harvard offered very good financial aid. Because Michelle has committed to working in primary care, a lesser-paying area of medicine, her debt may drop by $10,000 to $20,000.

Now thirty-four years old, Michelle is passionate about promoting wellness in low-income communities. She describes the opportunity as healing; it offers meaning as to why she had to endure such tough times as a child. Despite limited common ground surrounding life experiences and goals, family relationships for Michelle have become solid and loving. Hugs and "I love you" are the norm with her parents. Her mother, who found appropriate mental health treatment, has turned her life around in recent years. She calls regularly and makes an effort to keep up with Michelle's endeavors.

"My mom makes a point to write down the exact names of where I am and what I'm working on. I think she's the only family member who could tell you my major and minor in college!"

Michelle and her father have also become close over the years. Following her divorce, Michelle decided to expose her dad to a language other than "Iowan." After a visit, when it was time to say good-bye, Michelle hugged Mike and told him she loved him.

"The first time he looked at me like I was crazy," she says, "but ever since he's shown a lot more emotion. At my wedding, he gave an emotional speech that made him, and most of us, cry. He always hugs me when I see him and says 'I love you' when we finish a phone call. He's also made a lot of positive changes in his life. He quit smoking and bikes thirty to fifty miles a day. He told Jason that if I can get into Harvard and become a doctor, he should probably take responsibility for his health."

Nearly twenty years have passed since Michelle's high school guidance counselor snickered in the face of her dream. The counselor passed away never knowing that the student she thought was best suited for a factory job cleared every hurdle to becoming a doctor. Michelle won't take all the credit.

"There's so much that went into me getting where I am. Hard work, my attitude, and being smart are part of why I've gotten to do what I've done," she says, "but I've also had mentors come into my life at the right times or have had someone lend me money when I've hit rock bottom. I can't say for a minute that I'd be where I am without things like that."

The little girl with little support and little hope for a bright future saw the writing on the wall, and instead of finding an excuse, she found a way to rewrite her story.

"You're the only one who can decide to get out of bed in the morning and what you're going to do with your day. You can sit around thinking, *I have no choice*, but there's always another choice. It may not be something that's easy and that you want to do, but there's always more than one choice. Sometimes you just have to pick the hard one."

What fun it will be to watch the choices Dr. Hauser makes in the years ahead. They will no doubt better her life, and, if she achieves yet another dream, all of our lives, too.

I've been absolutely terrified every moment

of my life—and I've never let it keep me from

doing a single thing I wanted to do.

—GEORGIA O'KEEFFE

# ⇥ LAILA ALI ⇤

Laila Ali may have a famous father, but she's never liked coattails.

"I'm like the anti-celebrity," Laila says with a laugh. "I'd rather not be noticed."

But offer her a pair of boxing gloves, and she's all in.

"I've always been a fighter. I've always had everything it takes to be a fighter, but it took me a while to figure out how to channel that energy in the right place."

Laila is the youngest daughter of Muhammad Ali, considered one of the greatest athletes in boxing history. Her mother, Veronica, is Ali's third wife and was nearly fourteen years his junior when they married in Los Angeles, California. By the time Laila was nine, the marriage

*(Courtesy of Allen Cooley)*

ended; her mother was awarded custody of Laila and her older sister.

She describes her mother as loving but busy with social activities, trying to regroup after the divorce. Within a year, when Laila was ten, her mother's boyfriend moved in with them. Laila found him manipulative and domineering. She became angry with her mom for allowing the boyfriend's controlling behavior. The daily stress damaged the bond between Laila and her mother. She felt alone and rebellious. Her relationship with her father, who was battling Parkinson's disease, was caring but not close. She'd resisted his insistence that she be a "respectful Muslim woman" and embrace the teachings of his Islamic faith.

Angry and frustrated by a fractured home life, Laila got into the wrong crowd during her adolescence. She socialized with older kids, ignored her schoolwork, and even spent three months in a juvenile detention center.

That was a wake-up call.

Realizing she needed to redirect her life, fifteen-year-old Laila began attending beauty school after her high school classes. She soon found work as a manicurist in a nail salon. Laila then enrolled in a Santa Monica community college, moved out on her own, and while working toward a two-year business degree, opened a nail salon. She was eighteen and comfortable maintaining a low profile.

"Most of my clients," she says, "didn't even know my father was Muhammad Ali."

And then, with a click of a button, Laila's world changed. It was the night of March 16, 1996.

"I turned on the TV like everyone else to watch the Mike Tyson fight, and here come these women. I was totally surprised. *What is this?* I didn't even know women boxed. I thought, *I could fight and get paid for it without going to jail?*" She laughs. "I had my share of fights in high school."

In front of Showtime cameras in Las Vegas, the world got a glitzy glimpse of professional women boxers in the ring. Twenty-seven-year-old Christy Martin, promoted by Don King, was on Mike Tyson's undercard, the preliminary bout before the main event. Martin was fighting Deirdre Gogarty, a match that would put women's boxing on sports fans' radars. And one in particular.

"I immediately wanted to do it and I knew I'd do it well," Laila recalls. "I understood that I'd have to train hard and learn the skills, but I knew I would be able to become a champion with every cell in my body."

Except for that pesky little anti-celebrity cell. It balked at the idea of stepping into the public spotlight. The eighteen-year-old struggled with the inevitable trade-off.

"Am I going to follow my heart or am I going to let this

whole idea of fame and being a celebrity hold me back?"

The answer lay in rejiggering how she perceived fame. Instead of viewing it as a negative, Laila began to envision using a platform of success as a tool.

"I considered how many lives I could touch, people that I could inspire, how I could contribute to the world in a positive way."

And so, at age twenty, Laila hit the gym. She told people she was simply using a boxing regime to get into shape, quietly gauging whether she had the stuff that her head and heart told her she did. Laila knew better than to consult her body. In fighting shape? Hardly; not even close. The complete change in lifestyle would be physically shocking. She'd never worked out before or considered making the choices required of an athlete.

"Like most teenagers, nutrition wasn't my focus. I ate whatever I felt like eating: hamburgers and French fries and a lot of processed foods."

Everything had to change. She began working out two hours each day, six days a week, with the best available trainer at the boxing gym. Their challenge was two-pronged.

"It wasn't just training and working out," she explains. "It was learning a new skill at the same time."

Laila's trainer used focus mitts to teach her the basics

of punch combinations and technique. She worked the large, cylindrical heavy bag to get a realistic feel for landing punches; the resistance toned her muscles. A treadmill and jump rope improved her endurance. Within two weeks, Laila lost weight. She needed to drop at least twenty pounds to achieve a fighting weight of 165. With a daily calorie burn in the multi-thousands, she ate as much as she wanted of what was considered at the time to be healthy fuel.

"I ate pasta, steak, and potatoes—the old-school boxing go-tos."

Laila's body was changing. And screaming.

"When you're not used to using certain muscles that you didn't even know you had, it feels like you've been in a car accident. You're so sore and tight."

She was sparring in the gym mainly with men, developing the ability to overpower opponents with both her body and her brain.

"With boxing, you have to continue to keep thinking and making smart moves," she says. "You have to figure out a way to win the fight. Boxing is a very mental game."

Laila discovered she was gifted with the ability and drive to ignore—for the most part—the fear of getting punched in the ring.

"We go into the sport not thinking about the pain or getting hurt. It's hard to explain, but every time we get hit we don't feel it. Certain shots hurt, but not every time. It takes a certain type of person."

Laila's father, then living in rural Michigan, heard through the gym-rat grapevine that his daughter was sparring. When he came to town for a visit, he asked Laila if it was true. She confirmed the news and told him of her plans to go pro.

"My dad and I bumped heads for years because we're so much alike. So, he didn't try to say 'Don't do it' because he knew that wouldn't work, but he did try to bring up all the bad things that could happen in the ring: The whole world's going to be watching you. What if you get knocked down or knocked out? I just said, 'You've been knocked down, Dad, and you got up and kept fighting.' He was concerned about my safety, and," she adds with a laugh, "I think he wanted me to leave his legacy alone. He didn't want any of his kids coming behind him, embarrassing him, let alone his youngest daughter!"

After a year of training in the boxing gym, in October 1999 Laila was ready for her first professional fight. Her manager was her soon-to-be husband (and later ex-husband), whom she credits with expertly guiding her along the path to professional boxing.

"He was definitely good for that one thing." She laughs. "That was his purpose in my life."

At five feet eleven, one hundred sixty-six pounds, Laila began her professional career. The twenty-one-year-old knocked out her first opponent in less than a minute. Laila dominated in the ring from that match forward.

Warming up with trainer Roger Mayweather before the championship title fight versus Valerie Mahfood, Las Vegas, 2002 *(Courtesy of Laila Ali)*

In 2007, the twenty-nine-year-old ended her pro career with a flawless record: 24-0 with twenty-one knockouts (including the first female boxer she watched on television, Christy Martin, in 2003).

While Laila knew instantly that the boxing ring was where she belonged, the decision to fight professionally required a draining and daunting physical transformation, as well as a quick jab to her desire for privacy. She says ultimately, the result has been extremely rewarding.

"It's a feeling of accomplishment. It's a feeling of going as hard as you possibly could and not having regrets because you didn't try hard enough or because you had fear. Everybody's going to have an opinion, but you have to do what's in your heart."

In March 2015, Laila made a triumphant return to boxing, but this time as a television corner analyst for NBC's *Premier Boxing Champions*.

"To say my dad will be watching his baby girl on TV and beaming with pride," she says, "is an understatement!"

While boxing will always be her first love, Laila says she's very excited about sharing with people what she's learned through years of studying nutrition, fitness, and wellness.

"Many people aren't as informed as they could be about how to live a long, healthy life. African Americans are disproportionately affected by conditions such as obesity, diabetes, and heart disease, so it's an area where I feel like I can really make a difference. That is what fuels me now."

Sounds like another KO.

The person who risks nothing does nothing,

has nothing, is nothing, and becomes nothing.

He may avoid suffering and sorrow, but he

simply cannot learn and feel and change and

grow and love and live.

—LEO F. BUSCAGLIA

✦✦✦

# ❧ CRAIG AND KATHI ❧
# JUNTUNEN

San Jose, California, in 1964 smelled like freshly cut grass and homemade cookies. Kids played outdoors and neighbors were extended family. At least in the suburb where Craig Juntunen was raised.

"When I was a kid, I would go to my friend's house and they didn't have their door locked; I would never even knock on their door," Craig says. "I'd just show up and eat dinner over there. There was decency and a sense of proper behavior. Our neighborhood was absent of conflict and strife and divorce. We had Little League and PTA meetings and there was no turbulence in our world." He pauses. "Maybe there was, but it was hidden from us. There wasn't a burden of confusion for us, and that gave us an enormous sense of comfort and security."

"Us" was Craig and his brother, who was nine years older. Their parents, Jack and Josephine, married as teens and, because they were both somewhat shy, did everything together. The family's life revolved around the boys' busy sports schedules.

When Craig was ten, his teen brother left home to explore the popular counterculture movement. The remaining three Juntunens spent all their free time focused on Craig's passion for sports, primarily football. Because Northern California was less developed in the 1960s, the powerhouse San Jose Stingers had to travel great distances to compete against other schools in the Pop Warner league. That meant the Juntunens and other families were road warriors nearly every weekend of the football season.

"On Saturday, our parents would throw us into the car and we would drive nine hours to Eureka. At night, the parents would go to the hotel," Craig explains. "The kids would stay with families in Eureka. It was great. We had dinner with them, we'd get to know the kids we would be playing against, and we'd go to sleep. Then we'd get up the next morning, they'd serve you breakfast, we'd play the game, say good-bye, and then we'd disappear. That was the beginnings of where I learned how much fun it is to win, and how much fun it is to be part of a team."

Craig dreamed of one day playing Division I college football but hoped to grow taller and stronger in the years ahead. Always dwarfed by the rest of the peewee team, he had to work extra hard on other skills to make up for his small stature. Before dinner each night, Craig played catch with his dad to improve as a quarterback. Mr. Juntunen used his know-how as a mechanical engineer to build up Craig's throwing arm.

"He cut a little hole in the football and filled the football with sand. So, instead of the football weighing a pound, it weighed fourteen pounds," Craig explains. "We would play catch with this heavy football to strengthen my arm. We'd also play catch on our knees. It was really fun."

And it paid off. From 1969 to 1973, Craig started as quarterback for the Lynbrook High School football team. He was determined to reach his goal of playing college football.

"I wasn't a partier; I wasn't a runner with a bunch of girls. I always liked having one girlfriend. I'm one of the few guys in North America who never smoked pot. I never got thrown out of school. There wasn't any real edge to me as a kid because the focal point was that I wanted to go as far as I could with my sport. I was compromised as an athlete, and I knew the only way I had a chance to keep going was to not take chances and to maximize whatever limited talents I had."

Financial resources for the Juntunens were also limited. His mother and father both worked, but money for college would have to come by way of an athletic scholarship. Craig assumed that was the case but still remembers the Saturday afternoon when his father mentioned, as they routinely cleaned up the garage, that he had something to tell him.

"I thought he was going to say, 'We're having hamburgers tonight,'" Craig recalls with a laugh. "But he said, 'If you want to go to college you're on your own.' And I said, 'Okay, I got it.' I really admired the fact that he said it because I think it was hard for him. I think it was something that was eating at him for a while and he had to get it out."

Eighteen miles northwest of San Jose was Craig's dream team: the Stanford Indians (now the Cardinal). During high school, he made extra money on Saturday afternoons selling ice-cream malts at Stanford football games.

"I was a horrible malt salesman because I'd watch the game instead of selling malts," he admits, "but I dreamed of playing on that field. But that dream never materialized. I just wasn't good enough."

Members of the Indians football program encouraged Craig to try to improve his slight build at a junior college. He enrolled in De Anza College, a community school in Cupertino, California, from 1974 to 1975. To his frustration, Craig's efforts in the weight room were not effective enough. Playing football at Stanford would remain just a dream.

As Craig got busy looking for other college opportunities, serendipity got to work behind the scenes. In Moscow, Idaho, coaches for the University of Idaho Vandals were watching a recruiting film featuring the center for Craig's high school football team. But it was Craig's performance in the quarterback position that caught their eye. The staff liked what they saw and offered him a full ride.

"I remember when they called and offered me my scholarship. My father was right around the corner listening, and I said into the phone, 'I will accept this.' We high-fived and hugged; it was as if we had reached the top of Mount Everest together."

The U of I football program lacked the cachet of storied Stanford, but Craig was gratified that instead of dreaming about Division I football, he'd now be playing it. In 1976, he led the Vandals to a 7-4 record and a second-place finish

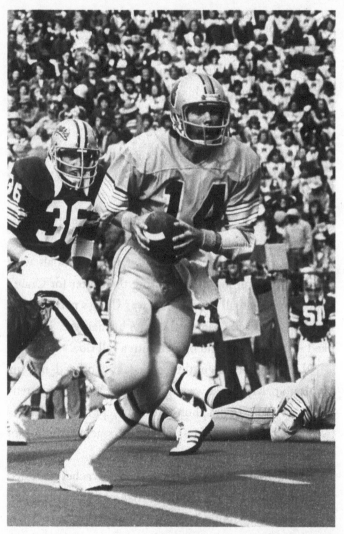

in the Big Sky Conference. He cocaptained the team in 1977 and won the offensive MVP award.

"Idaho was a great learning experience for me. It wasn't the big time relative to college football, but the basic experience is still the same," says Craig. "You have the camaraderie in the locker room, you're part of a team, there's a band of brothers, and you're working together to achieve a common goal. That was the real enriching part of the experience."

Craig's success on the college level paved the way for the next part of his dream: playing professional football. The National Football League in the late seventies was interested in tall pocket-passing quarterbacks. Because Craig was a relatively small running quarterback, he headed north to the Canadian Football League. In 1978, he was signed by the Calgary Stampeders as a quarterback. That same year he married the girl he'd been dating since high school. Together they moved from city to city as he was hired and cut by football teams.

In May 1980, Craig entered training camp to vie for a quarterback slot on the Hamilton Tiger-Cats. His two decades on the gridiron would come to an end; he was cut from camp. At twenty-five years old, Craig would now have to walk off the football field and begin pounding the pavement for another line of work.

The year before, during the off-season, Craig met a man who described to him the lucrative industry of head-hunting. Craig contacted the acquaintance and, in 1981, landed a headhunting job in Palo Alto, California. After just one year in the business, Craig decided to venture out on his own with a business partner.

That same year, he and his wife were divorced. "We were too young when we got married," Craig says.

Single and focused on his new career, Craig began to build a successful search business. His goal was to retire by age forty and enjoy a life of freedom and spontaneity, two things he valued greatly. He would consider marriage again but never saw himself having children. His limited exposure to kids was mentoring young football players who visited training camp during college.

"I always found that interaction to be enlightening and charming and fun, but then they went home at night," Craig says. "I saw the distinction between interacting with kids and then the burden of a twenty-four/seven operation. That to me looked overwhelming."

He also knew what good parenting looked like from his own upbringing and knew he lacked that level of dedi-cation.

"I don't like to be conflicted. I didn't want to be in a meeting in my office looking at my watch, especially knowing that my father would sneak out of work to watch me play. They sacrificed so much to go to stadiums to watch me play. It really was a remarkable thing that they did, and I didn't want to be the dad who didn't do that."

By 1985, Juntunen Inc. was lucrative and growing. Craig was thirty and dating a woman who was fully on board with a relationship that did not include having children. She and Craig discussed the option of his having a vasectomy.

"To me it was such an easy and simple solution that I said, 'Well, let's just do that.'"

Let's do that. Just like that. A vasectomy at thirty years old.

"I never gave it a second thought," he says. "It was literally no big deal for me."

Craig drove himself to the urologist. The doctor told him the procedure could include attaching a plastic hose with a valve in case Craig ever wanted to change his mind, or he could perform an irreversible vasectomy. Craig chose the simpler version.

"I remember the day I had the procedure and how incidental it was to anything. I just wanted to make sure my parts would still work in a few days. I was more concerned about missing a half day of work that day."

Twenty-five minutes later, Craig drove himself home,

limped up the driveway, watched a movie, and went to bed with peace of mind.

In 1988, two years after marrying the woman he'd been dating, Craig and his wife realized they were not meant to be a couple for life. He ended his second marriage and began his second divorce.

"I had this deal where I was a football star and fairly successful, but going through another divorce. I was questioning my attractiveness; maybe I had lost my touch," he explains. "It just felt like I should go out and date, but the dating thing was not fun. It was work and laborious. I had all these people set me up, and you know instantly when it's not right, and it's just a series of disappointments."

Work was also busy as Juntunen Inc. grew and prospered.

"It was a time in my life when I was around a lot of people, but I was extraordinarily lonely. I just felt really empty and shallow."

In 1989, after eight years in the headhunting industry, Craig felt that by diversifying the company's business model, Juntunen Inc. would become a more salable asset. His partner disagreed.

"Everybody thought I was nuts. I was suggesting something that had never been done before. There was a lot of resistance within my company. It wasn't necessary to take this risk; things were good. But I really felt there was an opportunity that supported going down this path."

The only way to resolve their different visions for the company's future was for Craig to execute a buyout. He took his parents to dinner to tell them that in order to secure the funds he needed for a buyout, he would have to put his own home and the home he'd bought for them on the line. Craig knew the risk required would not sit well with his father, a child of the Depression who understood how hard life could be amid excessive loss.

"I remember taking my parents to dinner and telling them, 'I'm going to buy my partner out and I think it's the right thing to do and it will allow me to have an exit strategy and retire on my plan.' My mom said, 'Go for it, son,' and my dad . . . my dad's eyes were like Slinkies that came out of his eyes. That just wasn't the way he thought because he knew how *bad* bad can be."

At the same time, Craig began dating an accomplished business executive named Kathi Adler, who was a vice president at a software company and responsible for more than $8 million in revenues. Before they ever went out on a date, the two had occasionally crossed paths after work in the weight room of the Decathlon Club in Santa Clara. Both were seeing other people and neither knew what the other did for work. But in 1989, Kathi ran into Craig in the lobby of his company. She was in search of a new job and needed a headhunter.

"I had no idea that he ran the company," Kathi explains. "I said, 'Oh, gosh . . . funny seeing you here! What do you do?' And he said, 'Oh, I do everything. I sweep the floors, I clean the bathrooms.' I just thought, *Oh, okay.* And then after my interview, I learned he was the president of the company. He wasn't my type at all, but I was so impressed by his humility and his demeanor that I thought, *He seems like a nice guy. Maybe I should go out with him.*"

In January 1990, Craig asked Kathi to lunch. Since his divorce, he was implementing an "honesty is the best policy" approach on first dates with women. It sounded like this:

"I am never going to get married again, and I had a vasectomy, so I will never have kids."

Awkward pause.

"They were stunned by my position," says Craig. "Like, 'Wait a minute—you seem like such a good, wholesome guy. And you don't want to have kids? You don't want to get married again?' But I wanted to get it over with. I didn't want it to come up months later. I think I was just exasperated and worn out from the whole dating thing." He was also still hurting from his two divorces. "I just didn't want to have to go through that again."

On his first date with Kathi, Craig stuck with the brutal-truth policy and unleashed the verbal hounds:

"I am never going to get married again, and I had a vasectomy, so I will never have kids." He threw in: "Don't count on me ever sending you flowers, because I don't believe in that."

No awkward pause this time.

"I actually just started laughing," Kathi says as she laughs again thinking back on the lunch. "I said, 'That's way more information than I need to know right now because this is really just our first date and I'm seeing other people. Thanks for letting me know.'"

Still, Kathi found Craig refreshing and fun. They soon discovered that they shared an enthusiasm for hard work and recreational sports.

"On our second or third date," Craig recalls, "she had to get something out of her car trunk and I followed her. She had a bat and a glove in there."

Kathi laughs. "I always kept sporting equipment in my car—baseball stuff or basketball stuff. That's just me—in case someone wanted to play a pickup game."

Craig's parents had kept track of his lively dating life following his divorce. So, after he met Kathi, he said to them, "I think I found one." He recalls, "I said, 'Mom, she had a bat and a glove in her trunk.' My mom said, 'She's a keeper.'"

Craig was thirty-five with two failed marriages, completing the buyout of his partner and restructuring Juntunen Inc. Kathi was thirty-one and had been married to a professional football player for five years. Both had high-pressure jobs but worked hard to carve out time for each other. Kathi got a glimpse of the pressure Craig was under when she spent the night at his house several months into their relationship. He rolled out of bed and "literally passed out." She says, "I was thinking, *Wow.*" She adds jokingly, "*Were things that great between us that I killed him?* But what really happened was that he was just under so much stress at that time with his business that he literally got up and passed out." (He came to within minutes.)

Kathi had worked hard for the life she'd built so far—an MBA from Northwestern University's Kellogg School of Management, a high-powered job, her own home—but she was falling in love with Craig. Six months after they began dating, they decided Kathi would move in with him. A small crack formed in the wall Craig had built up to ward off commitment.

"It's kind of like when a sunny day shows up," he says. "You don't question it; you just enjoy it."

By September 1990, the buyout was complete and

Craig began to bring to life his vision of diversifying Juntunen Inc. and making the company more effective for its customers. The business model was unique (at the time) to the headhunting industry and would target emerging technology companies, starving for personnel and productivity during the high-tech heyday of the early nineties. The concept was solid but would take time to flourish. Craig found that his fourteen years in the hard-knocks world of football helped him stay resilient in the face of frequent setbacks. He found, too, that the team-building skills he'd honed as a quarterback translated well into the management of his staff.

"We had a real culture of achievement. We did Outward Bound, rock climbing, white-water rafting, and ropes courses. We were always trying to deploy the very best of the human condition in the benefit of our customer and in the benefit of our company."

Still, the building process was taxing. The company nearly went broke one year into the restructuring.

"I used to tell people that once you own your own company you start to sleep like a baby. You wake up every hour crying," he says. "There was never any real relief as we got bigger, because we could have a victory in our Bellevue office but in our North Carolina office there was a crisis. There was always this corner of the attic that was on fire

and you had to deal with that fire quickly or the whole
house was going to burn down."

Even with seventeen straight quarters of company
growth, Craig found the lows in the corporate climate to
be more prominent than the highs.

"In football if you won, you could walk off the field,
relax, and enjoy the win for a few hours. But there were
only a few Fridays I remember driving home from the office feeling pretty good, feeling like a winner. Those were
few and far between. Most of the time," he admits, "I felt
discouraged and incomplete."

His relationship with Kathi was the bright spot. "She
was the positive energy behind a lot of this process."

The couple's relationship deepened. They shared a
vision of the future with each other and without children. While Kathi loved kids and babysat her nieces and
nephews for weeks at a time, she too would never have
biological children. Several years earlier, she'd developed an
infection in her reproductive organs that resulted in her
becoming infertile. Kathi felt fulfilled by her loving family,
good friends, stimulating career, and now her close relationship with Craig.

"We fell in love and we had a goal together and we
were the ultimate buddies," Craig says. "We were very
happy being consumed with each other. My goal was our

goal, which was to sell the company and become ski bums. I think all of us have a real desire to embrace and understand freedom, and that's what retirement is supposed to give you."

Kathi adds, "Both of us had similar backgrounds in that we were very focused from college on work; we never took vacations, we never went anywhere, we just worked. So, as we grew together and were becoming successful, we really dreamed about retiring at forty and being able to travel and not have so much stress every single day."

In October 1995, at forty, Craig sold Juntunen Inc. to Fort Lauderdale–based Interim Services Inc. for an amount that would allow him and Kathi to never work again. The eight months prior to the sale were exhausting; the process involved discerning which of three interested companies Craig would choose. He was clandestinely managing the potential acquisitions while also running the day-to-day operations of Juntunen Inc. He was physically and emotionally drained when the day of the sale, October fifth, finally arrived.

"It happened on a Thursday and we had everybody in the conference room, their lawyers and my guys. You would have thought I was selling IBM, they had so much paperwork," he recalls. "It was unbelievable how much stuff I had to sign. It took all afternoon. I remember when it was over, we all shook hands, and it was about eight o'clock at night. I took Kath to dinner and I thought it was going to be this huge celebration, but I was numb. I was tired; it was over. It didn't feel how I thought it was going to feel."

Plus, although Craig had finally completed a grueling marathon, the terms of the sale required that he run even farther. He had to stay on with the company for three more years to ensure a smooth transition. The new CEO had a more structured management style than Craig, so the company's cultural environment changed and his former employees struggled to adapt.

"If I was gone it would have been hard for me just to hear about it, but to live it was really hard," he says. "I was showing up for work without a whole hell of a lot to do. The last year was one of the worst years of my life."

Kathi stayed on and worked for the new company as well. Within a year of the sale, another transition: Craig asked Kathi to become his wife.

"When he did propose I was like, *Okay, I'm not giving him any time to change his mind*," she says with a smile. "I said, 'Can you get ready to get married within two months?'"

On October 5, 1996, exactly one year after the sale of the company, Craig and Kathi married. They were committed to each other and to their dual dream of one day doing what they wanted when they wanted. That day turned out to be October 10, 1998. At ages forty-three and forty respectively, Craig and Kathi officially retired. They said good-bye to work and hello to Hawaii for ten days to map out how the rest of their lives would unfold.

In May 1999, the Juntunens moved to Vail, one of their favorite places to ski, snowshoe, and hike. They spent all of their time together and with their beloved golden Labrador retrievers, Buster and Bubba.

"When we first retired," Craig says, "I woke up every morning pinching myself and giggling in the sense that I didn't have to deal with anything anymore, and it was such a sense of freedom. My morning ritual was walking our Labs past the golf course, and we'd go down to the creek and I'd wash my face in the water and we'd watch the sun come up over the Rockies. It was very peaceful and I felt really safe. I didn't understand how calm things could get, how slow things could get. It was very different from this whirlwind we had been on."

For fun, Craig went through a clinic to become a ski instructor and got hired for $9.00 an hour giving lessons at a local resort. Both young and healthy, Craig and Kathi also spent extended periods of time traveling the world. They voyaged aboard small cruise ships to Italy, Turkey, and Greece, where they biked, hiked, and explored.

Snowshoeing in Vail, 1999 *(Courtesy of Kathi Juntunen)*

"I had traveled the country for work," Kathi says, "but I had never traveled internationally, so those were just great days."

In 2000, it made sense for the active couple to buy another house, this time in Arizona, which allowed them to play golf when Colorado was less inviting.

"In the early days of retirement, we basically lived like a dog," Craig says. "There were the ritual undertakings—you slept, you ate, and you got a little exercise every day. The biggest decisions we made were, 'Are we going to use a three wood or a driver off the tee?' and 'Are we drinking red or white wine for dinner?' Life couldn't have been any easier for the first year."

There was abundance: recreation, travel, fabulous restaurants, and cocktail parties on the country club circuit. More of a homebody than Kathi, Craig tolerated the high-end gatherings and immersed himself in countless rounds of golf with friends. As a couple, they were very happy and rarely had any source of conflict. However, there were some adjustments. Craig was used to relying on support staff as CEO of a company.

"We had to work through that," Kathi says, chuckling. "He would scream my name out to come help him do something. I was like, 'Okay, time out.' That was a bit challenging."

But, in hindsight, Craig calls the allure of retirement one of life's greatest tricks.

"I think life does have to have purpose, and I think we do benefit from some sort of tension in our lives, to a healthy degree—some problem you're trying to solve, some piece of the puzzle you're trying to fit. I think the human condition likes to be challenged and intrigued. The problem with retirement is that most of what's in our forefront are memories of how it was. You're not looking forward to anything other than another round of golf or another party. There isn't anything that's pressing in front of you, so all the really good parts of your life are in the rearview mirror. We'd go to these cocktail parties and everybody was talking about what *used* to happen. We were very seldom talking about what we were doing tomorrow, because we knew what we were doing tomorrow— we were going to go to the golf course, play golf, have a few cocktails, and go to somebody's house for dinner . . . where we'd again talk about what we *used* to do," Craig says with a laugh.

In 2000, Kathi took a job at a family learning center teaching elementary school students. She also spent a month in Mexico volunteering at an orphanage. Opting out of the tight-knit country club lifestyle was delicate, but Kathi was feeling more connected with her Catholic

upbringing and less with what had become a rather un-
rewarding routine.

"It just began to feel a little narcissistic, a little too, *Is
this all we're going to do for the next forty years of our lives?*
Something didn't feel right."

Craig describes himself in the second year of retirement
as chronically empty rather than bored; conflicted, too.

"There was a period of personal mutiny going on because after all, this was the plan and we got there and it was
such a luxurious, and in many respects, such a good life," he
says, "so how could I question that?"

In August 2001, Craig was offered an intriguing opportunity that would take him back to a place where his most
gratifying memories were made—the football field. His college roommate, who had become the head football coach
at the University of Nevada, invited Craig to spend a week
observing players participating in the Wolf Pack training
camp. Craig agreed, and ultimately, his old friend valued his
insightful input. The coach then suggested to a colleague,
the head football coach at Arizona State University, that
Craig could offer fresh eyes on his football program, too.
By 2004, Craig had accepted a full-time job with the team
as director of player development and assistant to the head
coach. Staff members lightheartedly dubbed him the Archi-
tect of Attitude for his impactful relationships with players.

"I was a cross between a sports psychologist and a success coach. I usually had about seven or eight one-on-ones a day, and I'd have confidential conversations with the players. We'd talk about life—and football—and then I'd tell the coach patterns I was hearing from the team," Craig explains. "Then we did a whole bunch of character-development stuff in the off-season, things I learned in my business that I just contoured to football. I really loved it."

Kathi watched Craig flourish and rediscover a meaningful direction in life. She told him at dinner one night that she hadn't seen him as happy in years. Her own search was still under way.

"I was actually jealous. *My God, he got it! He found it!* It was a perfect blend of his skill sets—nurturing young men, football; he loves the whole team sports thing," she says. "I love sports, too, so it was a good thing for us as a couple. I really thought, *This is it*."

But was it? On a beautiful autumn morning in Arizona, a routine round of golf answered that question.

Craig knew of Rick Federico because they belonged to the same country club in Scottsdale. They'd shaken hands on the golf course but never shared a conversation. Rick was known as a community leader, a quality guy, and a very skilled businessman. He was also a successful fund-raiser for his alma mater, the University of Tennessee. In fall 2005, Craig received an e-mail from Rick asking if he'd like to be included in a threesome for Saturday golf. ASU had a bye week, so Craig agreed; it would be nice to pick Rick's brain about improving fund-raising efforts at ASU. That morning, the men decided to tee off on the back nine and soon began exchanging details about their personal lives. Craig beamed about Kathi. Then it was Rick's turn.

"I was intrigued by the way Rick spoke," Craig recalls. "He spoke from the heart."

Rick and his wife had raised three boys and took great pride in their kids' accomplishments and character. As Rick grabbed a six iron, he added that several years earlier, he and his wife had adopted two little girls from Haiti. Ting! He launched the ball into the middle of the green.

From that swing forward, the golf game for Craig took a backseat to his curiosity about Rick's "second" family. He'd never talked to someone about adopting, let alone from another country. He wasn't even sure where Haiti was on the world map. He asked Rick, "Do they call you Dad?"

Rick said yes.

"When he talked about his daughters he would tear up," Craig says. "This was not just something that he agreed to with his wife and he was a passenger on the ride. It was important to him. It mattered."

Craig next asked Rick why they adopted from Haiti. The answer was sobering. Rick explained that Haiti is the poorest country in the Western Hemisphere, where hundreds of thousands of orphaned children are starving and living in squalor. He added, "We probably should have adopted more."

Craig was transfixed and had countless questions for Rick. He learned that the Federicos used an agency that specialized in international adoptions, and they fell in love with a photo of the two sisters on a Web page. They flew to Haiti several weeks later to meet the girls and advance the adoption process. When Craig asked Rick if parenting adopted kids felt any different from raising his boys, Rick said, "Parenting is parenting. I loved it the first time, and the fact of the matter is I am doing a better job of parenting now than I did with the boys. Most of that is because I have more experience this time around."

The conversation stirred a sense of purpose in Craig that had been waiting, yearning for direction.

"The more he talked with me about Haiti, the more interested I was," Craig says. "That's when the train left the station: that day at golf."

On the drive home, Craig called Kathi and asked her

to make dinner reservations; he had something to discuss with her that night. All afternoon, he researched as much as he could about Haiti and an American priest Rick mentioned who had started a nonprofit organization in Haiti in one of the poorest and most dangerous slums in the world. At dinner that night, before their meals even arrived, Craig launched a verbal bomb downfield.

"I'm thinking about taking a trip to Haiti."

Across the table, Kathi responded as if he'd called the wrong play.

"I started laughing at him. It was kind of like that first-date lunch," she says, laughing again as she remembers the night. "*Really?* I said to him, 'Last time I checked, I don't think there's a Ritz-Carlton in Haiti.' That was so far out of Craig's element."

But she took a deep breath and let him explain his sudden interest in the western end of Hispaniola.

"I've learned over the years," Kathi explains, "to soft-sell my opinions a little more and to be more flexible. I won't dig my heels in; I'll try to ask some questions."

How would he travel there? Would he need inoculations? Were there safety concerns?

Craig didn't have details; he talked instead of the country's chaos and the desperate children in need of families, wandering the streets and struggling to survive.

By the end of dinner, Kathi was less skeptical and more interested in the idea of traveling to Haiti with Craig. But not just for him.

"Kath is extremely independent," Craig says. "There was something there for her, too."

Something that had always perplexed her.

"From the time I was young, I remember driving up the highway in California and watching migrant workers work in the fields," Kathi says, "and I would ask my parents, 'How did they get that life and I got my life?' The disparity in our world has always resonated in me. So, for me, getting to be involved with kids in Haiti? That would be incredible; I'd love to do that. It was just as much for me as it was for Craig and for us as a couple."

Over the next few days, Craig researched the country while Kathi looked into flights and hotels. Craig also scheduled an appointment for what he knew was inevitable but was extremely loathsome for his wife: shots.

"I am not a needle person. To this day, I can't even get Botox," she says with a laugh, "because the few times I've gotten it, I passed out."

Craig had to carry her out afterward, but Kathi toughed out the onslaught of six shots, protection against everything from typhoid to rabies.

That evening, Craig's continued fact-finding mission

online turned up a shocking and unexpected hurdle. The US embassy in Haiti had issued a high-severity travel warning and urged Americans to leave the country. Reasons for the warning ranged from well-armed gangs operating out of Port-au-Prince to ongoing security concerns, including "frequent kidnappings." When Craig called Rick for his thoughts, he suggested Craig e-mail the minister working in Haiti. Immediately, Craig took Rick's advice. The response back from Father Tom was disappointing. He confirmed that the security situation was indeed volatile and that the Juntunens should postpone their trip. Craig asked Kathi to come into his office; he had frustrating news to share, plus an idea to run by her. He told her of the trip-delaying travel warning, and then he dropped back again to throw a long ball.

"What would you say if I said I might want to adopt a couple of kids?"

A needle-weary Kathi did not mince words.

"You hate kids."

Craig insisted he did not.

Kathi began to cite evidence above and beyond the glaring exhibit A, his vasectomy. He refused to go to Disneyland with her. He threw his own tantrum when kids beside them misbehaved at restaurants. He barely survived Thanksgiving dinner with their nieces and nephews. She said she would love to adopt kids but felt it simply wasn't a fit for him. Craig politely disengaged. He decided he'd put Kathi through enough for now and that a fun trip was in order. He booked a suite at Kathi's favorite ski lodge in Deer Valley for the week ahead, in January 2006. Days before they left, Craig found a stack of paperwork on his desk with a note from Kathi. Next to a hand-drawn star on the top sheet she'd written: "This one looks good."

"It's typical Kath," Craig says. "She likes more information. She went and did her own research and then circled back."

She had researched international adoption organizations and agencies that specialized in placing children from Haiti.

"And it just so happened that one of the organizations I had given him was headquartered right outside Salt Lake City near where we were going skiing," Kathi says. "We both thought, *What are the odds of that?*"

Craig set up a meeting with the agency, which had overseen the construction six months earlier of an orphanage in a small village outside Port-au-Prince called Lamardelle. Twenty-two orphaned kids were housed there and the owners of the nonprofit had just begun matching approved families with children. Due to the months of travel warnings, they had not been to Haiti in more than a year. The owners told the couple that once travel restrictions were lifted, they would love to visit the orphanage with them. Before saying good-bye, the group stopped in the lobby to look at photos of children living in the orphanage. The Juntunens were captivated. They offered, once they saw the agency's credentials, to make a donation.

When Craig and Kathi got home, they decided to dabble in the process of potentially adopting children from Haiti. No matter what their decision, sorting through the required home study made sense.

In March 2006, two months after meeting with the Utah agency, Craig made plans to visit the crèche, Enfant de Jesus, with one of the managers they'd met. (In Haiti, a crèche is an orphanage that attempts to find families for its children. An orphanage simply houses children until they age out at sixteen.)

Based on their research before the trip, the Juntunens determined that Haiti still posed enough of a safety risk that Kathi should stay home. She made Craig promise to be extremely careful and not to bring home any kids.

"I remember being scared to go, but I went," Craig says. "I thought, *What if I get kidnapped? What's that like? What happens when you get kidnapped?*"

Craig flew from Arizona to Haiti through Miami. As the plane descended into Port-au-Prince, Rick's

description of the Caribbean island as "the poorest
country in the Western Hemisphere" dominated Craig's
thoughts.

"You know when you go to the doctor and the doctor
says, 'It's going to hurt,' and you don't know quite what that
means from a practical sense, you only know intellectu-
ally? Having your feet on the ground in a place like Haiti,
you appreciate how good we have it," Craig says. "You also
develop a real respect for how people are making the most
from the least. The Haitians are a really beautiful people
and very resourceful, and so the poverty doesn't erode any
of their dignity; in fact, if anything, it elevates their dignity
in how graceful their spirit is in these very harsh conditions."

From the time the plane landed, chaos ensued. The
airport terminal was beleaguered by equally high degrees
of humidity, noise, and incompetence. Craig eventually located his bags, which were loaded with toys, clothes, and
candy for the children. He and the agency's manager would
be accompanied to the crèche by two workers from Enfant de Jesus; one would serve as the interpreter, the other
their driver. Soaked with sweat, Craig rolled down the win-
dow of the gray pickup truck, only to choke on the putrid
smell of rotting layers of garbage. The logjammed streets
pulsed with a lunatic rhythm—pound the horn, slam the

brakes, repeat. Throngs of people were wheeling and dealing alongside the unruly traffic.

"There's just a real raw and almost organic gathering of life and decay, all smashed together," Craig describes. "Most of the commerce there is barter and trade. People are selling things everywhere. It's like one huge flea market in the streets of Port-au-Prince."

Eventually, the quartet made its way out of town and onto less-traveled roads pocked with potholes. The driver stopped at a small store with an armed security guard to buy a five-gallon jug of water for his passengers. He then turned off on a dirt road comprised of more rocks than dirt. When they finally bumped and banged their way into Lamardelle, Craig's travel partner suggested a brief walk through town. A narrow path offered a winding tour of makeshift houses with no electricity. A cement trough that ran along the roadside held the precious yet much compromised water supply. The multiple uses were horrifying—drinking, bathing, laundering. Farm animals had full access to the trough as well. Villagers bade the foursome hello in Haitian Creole and watched them wander through their neighborhood. En route back to the vehicle, Craig noticed another parked truck that had somehow dumped its load of pigs. The dirty herd was milling about and several were mating, thrusting other pigs into a jealous rage. Craig was on one side of the mayhem, the gray truck was on the other. He was forced to dart and dodge his way through a squealing, smelly crush of hogs.

"That was the most dangerous part of the whole trip!" Craig says, laughing.

When they arrived at the crèche, a massive metal gate forced them to idle and wait for permission to enter the four-acre compound. Armed guards looked down on the truck from a tower built next to the crèche.

"Inside those walls is sustenance and desperate people really want it," Craig explains, "whether it's a bag of rice or a chicken or whatever it may be. The guards are protecting the kids, but mainly the environment."

As the truck rolled through the gates, Craig saw a stark difference from the barefoot children he'd seen in the primitive village amusing themselves with a stick. The play yard at the crèche was active with clean-clothed children jumping rope and laughing as they kicked balls back and forth. The fourteen-thousand-square-foot building that housed the kids was constructed with cement blocks, a fortress for its innocent occupants. The orderly, happy environment was a welcome relief to Craig, who was still processing his first glimpse of the third world. Craig was introduced to Gina Duncan, a native Haitian who was educated in and also worked in the United States for years. Frequent trips to Haiti compelled her to move back and try to improve the lives of orphaned children. She had married a Haitian man named Lucien, and together they ran the crèche. Craig was impressed by the clean, efficient nature of the facility, complete with a preschool, large kitchen and eating area, laundry room, and sleeping quarters. The twenty-two children in the crèche were tucked in each night by staff they referred to as aunties. Craig decided to ease his way into the crowd of children playing, eager to join in if welcomed. A little girl in a red dress and white shoes walked over to meet him. As they strolled together she reached up and grabbed Craig's hand. His heart melted; the "kid guy" in him was revealed.

"I think he was always in there. I think as I have grown and evolved, whatever tiny part of being a kid guy just grew and blossomed over time. Seeing those kids there was so— it's hard to explain, but it was such a convergence of so many things for me," he says. "It was the contrast to the childhood that I had, and the other thing that really struck me was all the magic in these kids. But how was it going to come out? How were they going to evolve and grow and become who they were supposed to become?"

The little girl's name was Esperancia, which in Haitian Creole means "hope." Gina told Craig that Esperancia was four, and that she and Lucien had found her in a

mountainside village when she was a malnourished two-
year-old. Her mother was a single parent raising seven or
eight other children and allowed the Duncans to take Esperancia to their crèche. No family had shown interest in
adopting her during the two years she lived there. Craig
was amazed, and also floored by a whimsical little kick step
Esperancia did as she walked hand-in-hand with Craig. It
mirrored one that Craig sometimes did for Kathi as they
walked their Labs early in the morning, when sleeping
neighbors would not see his ambulatory antics. Was it a
sign that Esperancia was meant for them?

Craig continued to play with the children, who were
friendly and eager to have Craig teach them how to throw
a Frisbee. When the aunties called in the children for dinner, Craig took the opportunity to e-mail Kathi to let her
know that he was safe and to share some details about his
journey so far.

*The first thing that comes to my mind is how disappointed I am*
*that you are not here to share this experience with me . . . but it*
*has been an unbelievable day.*

He told her how the crèche and its staff exceeded his
expectations and that he'd already connected with a little
girl who miraculously did his "cartoon walk."

*I don't want to jump the gun, and I know we said that I would*
*not identify any kids for us to adopt unless something unique*
*came up . . . but . . . I don't know if I have seen anything more*
*unique. Can you be thinking what I am thinking . . . I have to*
*wonder if Esperancia is supposed to be our daughter.*

Of the twenty-two children in the crèche, half had
been matched with a family but were waiting for paperwork to be completed. By the end of that year, 310 children
would be adopted from Haiti through agencies, but an
estimated 380,000 orphaned children lived in the country.
The next morning, Craig noticed a charismatic boy named
Amelec in the play yard. He seemed bright and brought
real energy to the crèche. While Gina called the kids for
breakfast, Craig logged on to the facility's computer to
check for a response from Kathi.

*First of all I am glad you are safe and I, too, am disappointed*
*that I am not sharing this experience . . . and to think that*
*little girl did the fancy walk, maybe she has been waiting for*
*you. I will totally trust your decision, so if she is the one, I am*
*thrilled.*

It was important to Kathi that Craig make the decision first to adopt. She found in their relationship that

when he initiated a plan, the results were far more positive than when he felt something was being forced upon him.

That morning at breakfast, Craig asked Gina how to start the process of adopting Esperancia. He spent the next few days going with her to preschool and playing in the yard. Sitting next to her one night at dinner, he was quite impressed with all of the children's manners and polite demeanor. Craig also spent time with Amelec, who appeared to be naturally athletic and loved throwing the ball back and forth. Gina told Craig that Amelec's grandparents had dropped him off at the crèche two and a half years earlier and that he was now five years old.

"When I found out he was available, I thought, *He isn't any longer,*" Craig says. "We played catch together and I think it was the first time he'd ever played catch. It was really fun; we just connected."

It was time to e-mail Kathi again. He had more big news.

*I spoke to Gina this morning and you have a daughter. I also have some other news—we also have a son. Remember that kid Amelec I was telling you about? Well, I was shocked but Gina told me he is available. Apparently he has a horrible picture on the web page and no one has taken him. You will love this kid. He is stocky-athletic and a winner. He has a face full of energy and emotion. If you are really adamant and you need some time*

*about this we can find a way to put this on hold, but I think you*

*are just going to have to trust me on this one. I love you and you*

*will be the best mom any kid could have. I have known that for*

*17 years.*

One month away from turning forty-eight, Kathi was about to be a mother of two, sight unseen.

"Craig is my partner, so even though I wasn't there, I was there; not physically, but every other part of me was there," Kathi explains. "We were sharing our hearts together; we were just thousands of miles apart."

Gina invited Craig to visit several orphanages in Port-au-Prince so he could appreciate the unique and special aspects of Enfant de Jesus. But before they went to an orphanage, she brought Craig to the city's general hospital for a tour of the ward for abandoned children. He was repulsed. Deranged and deformed children screamed with little hope for comfort. The filthy ward was riddled with flies and horrific sights that so unnerved Craig that he didn't even remember their return to the parked truck.

"It just rattled me. You want to talk about something on the fringe of humanity—and everybody was just accepting it. That's what really got to me with everything,"

Craig says. "There seemed to be this general attitude that this is the way it is and we have to live with it."

Next, an orphanage. Shocked and sickened, Craig couldn't wait to leave. The facility was jammed with hungry children who were offered no comfort or stimulation. When Gina saw a young girl there who was supposed to be signed over to Enfant de Jesus, she became irritated. She told Craig they were going to pay a visit up the street to the monsignor who had gone back on his word. It was there that Craig saw a newborn baby swaddled in a blanket and propped up against the wall in a corner. The baby looked pale and sickly. Craig noted that despite a rash across his forehead, the baby's face was sweet and his eyes were alert. The monsignor said the infant had been found on a nearby doorstep and brought to the orphanage, which was ill equipped to care for older kids, let alone a newborn. Gina picked up the baby, hugged him, and handed him to Craig. She told him to go to the truck and she would complete the paperwork necessary to transfer the infant to her crèche.

"When we rode home that late afternoon," Craig recalls, "he held on to my thumb for dear life. He was really sick, but he wouldn't let go. I knew that kid was a fighter."

When they walked into the crèche, the staff hovered over the baby, dressed him in soft pajamas, and began

calling him Little Craig. After dinner, Craig e-mailed
Kathi about his extraordinary day and how Gina rescued
Little Craig.

> *Gina thinks he has a really good chance of surviving now that*
> *he is here. I know you have said all along that you don't want*
> *an infant, but this is a magical kid.*

"On the third or fourth day," Kathi says, "when I got
the e-mail about the baby—because keep in mind, this is
a guy who wouldn't come with me to babysit my nieces or
nephews, he wouldn't go to a restaurant and sit next to kids,
he just wasn't a kid person—I thought, *Oh my gosh. He has
no idea what he's getting involved with.* I was close to fifty
and he was fifty-one. I didn't have my own babies, but I've
been around a lot of babies, and they're a ton of work. That
was the only one where I said, 'You need to come back and
we need to talk about the baby.'"

The next morning, over a quiet breakfast, Gina told
Craig she felt the baby belonged to him and Kathi. Craig
wasn't startled. He felt in his heart it was true. But he told
Gina that he'd promised Kathi he would not adopt a baby.
Gina told him that sometimes things just defy logic and
then got up from the table.

Craig's emotions were in overdrive. He was being

exposed to so many things that were the extreme opposite of the life he'd been living one week earlier.

"I was shrinking. I was mentally and emotionally in complete atrophy, and then here I was thrust into this environment that was so stimulating," he says. "There was so much to consider and to think about—it was the opposite of going to one of these muted cocktail parties where we were all on autopilot. My emotions and my thinking about everything were electric. It was like all these lightning bolts going off."

Craig and Kathi exhausted their computer keyboards hashing out the potential adoption of a baby. In the end, they agreed that Little Craig, whom they renamed Quinn Lucien Juntunen, was meant to be part of their new family. His blood test came back clean, which meant the adoption could go forward.

"We had no idea about the certainty of any of these kids," Craig says, "but we agreed and committed to love them under any circumstances, which is the exact same platform that a parent who gives birth to kids goes into parenting with. Kathi and I felt we were going to love these kids and give them whatever we could to offer them the best chance at a productive life. Whatever was compromised . . . that to us didn't enter into the equation. Our plan was to give these kids what they didn't have, which was love and encouragement and role models. When I look back, the greatest gift my parents gave me was the gift of encouragement."

Gina and Lucien told Esperancia and Amelec that Craig was their new dad and that they would soon meet their new mother.

*It was one of the most special and memorable moments of my life. They were both so happy and excited. I love you, Kathi, and the fact that we are now going to raise these kids together. Sleep tight, baby. I will be dreaming of you and our new family and all that lies ahead.*

By summer 2006, Craig and Kathi had been to Haiti several times to visit the kids, waiting for the wheels of international adoption to turn and allow their family to begin life under the same roof. Kathi's initial trip to Haiti exposed her to the poverty and anguish Craig had described in his e-mails.

"We were doing a tour of the village and I saw this mom meticulously making these little patties," Kathi says, "and I didn't know what they were. I asked her through a translator what she was making. She said, 'They're dirt pies—mud pies.' I asked her why. She said, 'If my children are going to die because I can't feed them, I'd rather them die on a full stomach than an empty stomach.' That just really, really hit me."

When she arrived at the crèche to meet their kids for the first time, Kathi had an unexpected rocky start with Esperancia.

"In her little mind—the mind of a four-year-old— she had this whole vision of her dad and her and maybe a brother, but there was no picture of me in that little dream," she says with a laugh, looking back. "So, when she saw me for the first time, she took one look at me and started crying, like, *Who are you and why are you in my world?*"

The next visit went smoothly. Espie, as they called her, warmed up to Kathi and the almost-family-of-five continued to learn about one another and all the moving parts required to develop love and trust. Saying good-bye after each visit was not easy on any of them.

"It was confusing for Espie and hard on Amelec," says Craig. "He was devastated. I've never heard a kid cry like that. They had a hard time with trust right from the get-go because, who can they trust? The nannies in the orphanage came and went, so there were no real constants in their life other than the kids who were around them."

It took twenty-six hundred miles and seventeen years for Kathi to meet Craig the Kid Guy. The crèche offered her a look at him so seemingly far out of his element and yet so completely in it.

"It was really neat to see that side of him," she says, "and to see how great he was with all the kids—not just our kids. I hadn't seen that side so it was like seeing a new person."

The couple did all they could to ready their Scottsdale home for the kids' eventual arrival. Kathi decorated rooms for Amelec and Espie; Quinn would sleep in a crib in their room. The couple took control of what they could, like gathering educational toys and filling the closets with clothes. The rest was at the mercy of the meandering international adoption process.

"In this period of their lives, we knew how important these days were for the kids' developmental cycle," Craig says. "It was really frustrating for us because we had reading tools for them and reading games and all the things we thought would help them. We played with them with that stuff while we were there, but when we left, that stopped."

The physical trappings of raising kids were in place. But Kathi was quietly concerned about her and Craig's parenting style as a couple. They hadn't discussed a strategy and had shown signs in the past that they had conflicting approaches. Before they were married, Craig was out of town on a business trip and Kathi was staying at his house taking care of the Labs, Buster and Bubba. The house sat on thirty acres and Craig felt the dogs should not be allowed to sleep inside. But when he called to say good night to Kathi, he realized she felt differently. "I heard one of the dogs barking," Craig recalls, "and I said, 'I thought you were in bed.' She said, 'I am in bed.' I asked, 'Well, who's lying next to you?' And she answered, 'That happens to be one of your Labs.'"

With dogs, the lenient-versus-strict philosophical battles were amusing. Children were children.

"I never doubted that he would be a great dad," Kathi says. "It was, *How as a couple will this change our relationship and how will we parent as a couple?* That was more my underlying worry."

On August 20, 2006, it was game on. The call came that Kathi and Craig had been waiting five months to answer. Passports and visas were issued for the children and it was time to fly to Haiti to pick them up and bring them home for good. Within days, Kathi and Craig landed in the Caribbean and reunited with Amelec, Espie, and Quinn. Their first on-the-clock job as parents was flying with a four-year-old, a five-year-old, and an approximately five-month-old baby to Scottsdale through Fort Lauderdale. Imagine the challenge; a plane ride was as familiar to Amelec and Espie as a ride in a space shuttle for Craig and Kathi.

The brain tends to skip over details when it dreams of "one day," and that was the case for the Juntunens when they romanticized the final trip home with their children. Now every component of the trip was playing out in real time: the security lines, the cumbersome kid paraphernalia, the language barrier. How do you explain that a seat belt is not a toy when you don't speak Creole? How do you ask about the scary sounds the plane is making if you don't speak English? The flight from Haiti and the overnight stay in Fort Lauderdale delivered a smorgasbord of tribulations that most parents experience: vomit, diarrhea, sand in all the wrong places, air traffic delays.

"I remember lying in bed in the hotel room—and I've never had this happen in my entire life—I was hyperventilating and I could not breathe," Kathi says. "It hit me. *What have we gotten ourselves into?* I was petrified."

By the time the group landed in Phoenix, a forty-minute drive home in the dark remained. A newly hired nanny picked them up; she would stay for a few months to help with the transition. As they drove out of Phoenix on an overpass that showcased the downtown skyline, a galaxy of twinkling lights—but not in the heavens—amazed the kids.

"They looked out on the horizon and saw all these lights from the city," Craig recalls, "and they had no idea what that meant. They could have been on Mars for all they knew. There was so much sensory stuff and then there was all this doubt. Like, *Okay, is this real and can I trust this?*"

When the sun rose, nothing felt easy or went smoothly. The excited dogs scared the daylights out of the kids. Amelec mistook his closet for the bathroom. The intriguing dimmer switches got a workout. Untangling any snag—like Espie's not liking her meal—was tricky using hand signals.

"There are tension points in any day where effective communication helps redirect the course, and if you can't really communicate quickly, course correction becomes more of a challenge," Craig says. "Also, forget about us. Can you imagine the kids? Everything was new: television, hot and cold running water. They came from a very primitive environment and overnight they were beamed up to this new way of living with all this new stuff. What I learned is how unbelievably resilient kids are; at least ours were. They were intrigued by everything and intimidated by nothing. I'm sure they wanted to know more about how things were working, but they just accepted it all as a new way."

The shock and awe was more debilitating for Mom and Dad. They had given the nanny the first few days off to make the setting less confusing for the kids.

"I remember one time in the first three or four days," Kathi says, "Craig and I could barely get breakfast on the table without it being stressful. We looked at each other and said, 'How do people have jobs and have kids?!' We couldn't even get breakfast served."

They decided right away to ditch the extensive "family fun" activities they had planned on paper . . . before they could truly understand the live version of 2 + 3. A low-key routine now made more sense. The five hung around the house, visited the zoo, and tooled about in golf carts.

But on day ten, it was time for Amelec and Espie to not just dip their toes in the ocean of newness but to dive in headfirst. Because it was late August 2006, school in Arizona was already under way. Before the adoption was official, Craig and Kathi had spoken with specialists, done extensive research, and ultimately decided to enroll the two kids in a private school and see how they fared. Espie would be in pre-K, Amelec in kindergarten. How would they communicate? Would they fit in with the other students? Very quickly, Craig and Kathi knew they had made the right choice.

"It was amazing how they adapted and how much they

enjoyed it," Craig says. "And then it dawned on us that we had taken them out of an environment of being around kids, and that's all they knew—being part of this army. When we brought them home it was just us and the three of them. What we didn't appreciate was that not only was the functional living space different, but also the daily dynamic of being around kids."

The first week of school included some expected rough patches: hot and cold reactions to the school experience and some missteps. Kathi decided that Amelec needed a belt for his school pants. She threaded it through his belt loops and secured the buckle. Amelec loved it and was excited to wear the belt to kindergarten. At lunchtime, the Juntunens' phone rang.

"We got a call from the principal saying Amelec had an accident," Kathi says. "We were so shocked because that was not like him. We thought, *Oh my God! Is he reverting back to toddlerhood?* Everything went through our heads. When Craig went to go pick him up and bring him a change of clothes, in his broken little English he said, 'I knew I had to go to the bathroom but I couldn't get my belt off.'" She laughs. "Every day there were probably three or four of those kind of incidents."

Ironing out each day's wrinkles was exhausting; plus, Quinn was not sleeping much. There was also the tug-of-war between Craig and Kathi over time-outs and teaching moments.

"There's that old saying, 'There are no bad kids, there are just bad parents,'" Craig says. "I really believed we had this enormous opportunity and responsibility to influence all the things that were going to shape our kids' lives. That became a real source of tension for me and Kath once we became parents."

Why, then, would the couple add another plate to the full set already spinning above them? They simply could not forget the other children left behind at Enfant de Jesus.

Initially, the Juntunens thought they would simply help fund the crèche, but after months of interacting with the facility, they wanted to get more involved and attempt to advance the quantity and quality of adoptions. Just one month after the kids came home, Craig and Kathi began to research what it would take to create a nonprofit foundation in Haiti called Chances for Children. The goal was to partner with Enfant de Jesus to fund and manage the crèche, and to also improve the surrounding community.

"Not only did we have this very steep learning curve about how to be effective parents with children who don't speak our language," Craig says, "now we were getting into the nonprofit center of adoption in a country we had visited a few times but had very little knowledge about how the inner workings of that country operated. That learning curve was also very, very steep. That was mostly Kath. We would put the kids to bed and she would go down to the office and try to figure things out."

By September 2007, the foundation received its tax-exempt status. Kathi would eventually handle the day-to-day management of the crèche and Craig would focus on fund-raising. Their partners at Enfant de Jesus in Haiti continued heading up operations for the first six months so the couple could get into a routine with the kids.

"It's sort of a blur. I remember it was difficult," Kathi says. "Fortunately I'm a really solid sleeper. I need a minimum of six hours; I prefer eight. But when I do sleep, I sleep."

Over the next year, the children flourished, and the more Amelec and Espie heard and spoke English, the easier communication became. Craig's golf buddies, shocked by their friend's domestic transformation, encouraged him to write a book. They felt the amusing stories he'd shared with them about being a newbie parent at fifty-one would result in a good read. Craig considered the idea more of a chance to motivate a prospective parent to adopt.

"My deal was I had to write an hour a day," Craig says. "A lot of times that hour of the day would be in the middle of the night when I'd get up to go to the bathroom, like all old guys do."

In April 2009, *Both Ends Burning* was published. The name referred to a phrase his mother used when she felt overwhelmed, as he did in his role as a new dad. All proceeds from sales went to Chances for Children. For Craig, an intriguing result of his book was the reaction from readers who shared their own challenges with the international adoption process. Craig discovered that the Juntunens' cost and time frame for adopting was minimal compared to the average attempt. Families were spending $28,000 and waiting three to five years to officially adopt. Craig was alarmed and confused. Why would the system discourage the uniting of compassionate people with desperate children? He was also shocked by a steady decline in international adoptions over the past five years. He assumed there was simply insufficient demand in the United States to adopt children living in harsh conditions abroad.

To gather more information, Craig commissioned several studies to examine the process and the involved agencies, like the US State Department and UNICEF. He also founded Both Ends Burning, a nonprofit corporation to promote adoption everywhere and to facilitate improvements in the international adoption process. When more than a year's worth of research was completed, the data

Espie, Craig, Quinn, Kathi, and Amelec,
Scottsdale, 2014 *(Courtesy of Cameron & Kelly Studio)*

confirmed what readers of his book had already expressed: desire indeed existed at both ends, but multiple factors were obstructing an affordable and timely miracle in the middle.

"The problem was not that there weren't plenty of kids who needed a family, and not that there weren't plenty of families who wanted to adopt those kids," Craig says. "The problem was: how do you process the adoptions and get these kids home in a safe and predictable way? The process was so arbitrary. The entire system from a general operational perspective gave me cause for concern."

For three years, Craig and Kathi watched their own kids grow and flourish in the safety of their family. It was a heartbreaking reminder that millions of other children around the world—and the families who wanted them—were being denied a similar opportunity.

"Twenty or thirty thousand dollars just to engage in the adoption process?" Craig says. "It's one of the things we really wanted to look at and change. For us, the meaningful things that we did with our kids were not dependent on or related to any economic condition. What mattered to them was belonging to a family, knowing that they were safe and that somebody loved them."

Craig found that the whole ball of wax—all the factors that contributed to a flawed international adoption process—was as big as the globe itself. Some of the challenges:

- Child welfare services were basically nonexistent in many countries. Orphaned children simply did not count when it came to government priorities.

- International aid organizations sought to treat specific problems children encountered, like poor nutrition, malaria, and AIDS, but there seemed to be no concerted effort to place orphaned children into families.

- Well-meaning existing treaties instead added more bureaucracy and steps to the international adoption process and did nothing to compel governments to solve the problem of children living outside of parental care.

- Despite countless success stories, the very few cases where adoptions had gone seriously wrong grabbed the headlines. No organized campaign existed to counteract the negative publicity and set the record straight.

- Each country had a unique system for processing international adoption cases, yet they were all basically doing the same things. Standardized procedures could simplify and significantly speed up adoption case processing and lower the cost of adoption.

Craig identified social entrepreneurship as a catalyst for positive change. He felt that over the next decade, the same innovative approaches and can-do attitude that delivered productivity and performance in the private sector could be applied to the current global bureaucratic mess. While Kathi, through Chances for Children, was affecting change day to day on the ground level, Craig knew that Both Ends Burning had to take on the big-picture goal of making people aware of a crisis that was oceans away. They would then, ideally, pressure lawmakers to reform the adoption process.

"The reason political apathy persisted was that very few people knew about this issue," he explains. "We didn't have any social force with our leaders. Our government and all democracies have this condition where the leaders don't do anything proactively. It's a very reactive system, and what they react to are the squeaky wheels—lobbyists or concerned citizens. So there was no social awareness or concern to make this issue a political priority."

Craig began contacting people who'd successfully caused cultural sea changes. He spoke with Candy Lightner, who founded Mothers Against Drunk Driving, and

Nancy Brinker, the founder of Susan G. Komen for the Cure. Both women told Craig that social revolutions start in living rooms and grow from there. They also told him that they worked tirelessly for seven-plus years—without the benefit of today's social media—before their causes showed signs of becoming vast movements. Craig was also interested in creative ways to motivate people, so he researched the impact of cause-related documentaries like *The Cove,* about dolphin slayings in Japan, and *Waiting for "Superman,"* about the flawed American public education system. When Nancy suggested that he make a film, Craig decided to executive-produce a feature-length documentary about the plight of children languishing in orphanages overseas.

In August 2010, Craig flew with a film crew to Guatemala, Ethiopia, and Haiti to capture the joys and frustrations of several families attempting to adopt children. The crew also shot footage in Vietnam. Craig says his colleagues were a perfect example of how awareness can trigger action.

"The film crew knew nothing about this issue," he says, "and the more they learned, their trajectory of being originally curious, and then concerned, and then outraged was similar to mine."

Craig wanted the film to serve as a tool for change.

Here's where we are; now how do we fix it? The documentary was titled *Stuck*, to describe the plight of millions of orphaned children around the world.

In May 2012, a board member of Both Ends Burning arranged for a screening of *Stuck* at the exclusive Soho House in Los Angeles, where media moguls and celebrities gather to watch independent films and discuss them over dinner.

"In the audience that night were a number of people in the film business," Craig says, "and one of them was Meyer Gottlieb of Samuel Goldwyn Films. Afterwards, I went up to Meyer and he said, 'I really admire what you're doing, but your film has a lot of work to be done.'"

Based on Meyer's input and his own gut instincts, Craig reworked the film. It paid off. By fall 2012, *Stuck* had won several awards at prestigious film festivals.

Craig called Meyer and asked for a second viewing. He agreed and invited Craig to his private screening room.

"There were maybe ten chairs, and his chair was in the back and I was in the front row. We watched the film, and when the lights came back on I turned around, hoping he was still there," Craig says, laughing. "He said, 'That's well done, Craig; it's a lot better.'"

Weeks later, the men talked about how to best showcase

*Stuck.* As president of Samuel Goldwyn Films, Meyer agreed to distribute the film and suggested screening it in twenty test markets. Craig felt instead that a town-hall-meeting approach might better ignite a social movement—the living room approach that Candy and Nancy utilized. Craig scrambled to create a bus tour in February 2013 that would stop in sixty cities over seventy-eight days. The side of the bus would be plastered with the slogan "More than a movie. It's a movement."

"I felt we had a secret weapon, and that was volunteers across the country who would help make the event in their city a success, and because there are people who care about making wrong things right, by the time the tour started we had six hundred volunteers, and when the tour ended we had almost a thousand," Craig says. "It was an unbelievably magical experience because we had so many good people in this country who went out of their way to help."

After every screening, Craig moderated a question-and-answer session. He then wrapped up the evening with these words:

"'You may choose to turn your back on these kids, but from this point forward you can never again say you don't know.' That's how I said good night, every night."

The bus tour was timed to end in May 2013, while Congress was still in session. Craig and people from thirty-seven different states marched on Capitol Hill to make lawmakers aware of the need for change in the international adoption process. Ideally, the march would signify the first stirrings of a sustainable social movement.

The years since the Juntunens adopted were a whirlwind of raising kids and fighting for kids. Kathi spent about twenty hours a week focusing on ways to support and improve Enfant de Jesus, but Gina and Lucien handled 90 percent of the daily grind in Haiti; the goal was to eventually put the local couple in complete charge of the crèche. Craig and Kathi were constantly busy fund-raising for their respective charities, Chances for Children and Both Ends Burning. The hunt for donations was complicated.

"We have the same friends," Kathi explains. "We know the same people. Fund-raising is very challenging. It's very difficult. It creates another level of tension between Craig and me."

By the middle of 2009, for her marriage and for her kids, Kathi was ready to opt out of any new projects in Haiti.

"I literally said to the Duncans, 'This is probably our last year.' I was thinking, *Okay, life is going to get back to normal again.*"

But in January 2010, Earth's tectonic plates had a different plan. A catastrophic 7.0-magnitude earthquake hit sixteen miles west of Port-au-Prince, annihilating the city's poorly constructed residences and commercial buildings.

"The minute I heard that," Kathi says, "I knew it was going to be horrendous."

More than one hundred thousand people died, and millions already living in desperation were dealt another heaping pile of hardship.

Kathi's first priority was to somehow rescue the twenty-two children living in Enfant de Jesus who were waiting out the adoption period. She knew the container of food that had recently been shipped to Haiti for the crèche would be stuck in port and looted. Immediately following the earthquake, humanitarian visas were issued by the US and Haitian governments to allow several hundred orphans who were paired with American families—but whose paperwork was not yet approved—to be airlifted out to Florida. Kathi knew the Haitian government was fickle and began scrambling to coordinate air transportation as soon as possible. Complicating her efforts were downed communication systems in Haiti and constantly changing rules and direction from Haitian officials. A US Army rescue team airlifted the unharmed children from Lamardelle to the Port-au-Prince airport, where Kathi was desperately trying to coordinate a charter flight to pick them up.

"It was the most stressful period of my whole life,"

she says. "I remember the kids coming home from school one day and I had three phones going at the same time—a satellite phone, my cell phone, and a landline—talking to three people trying to orchestrate this."

Thankfully, the charter company she was corresponding with allowed Kathi to board the orphans on the return leg of a flight that was transporting an American businessman sent by his company to do emergency banking work in Port-au-Prince.

"The person who went in my place texted me and said, 'The banker just got on the plane and he has the hugest metal attaché case I've ever seen. He said it's filled with cash!'"

To Kathi, the most precious cargo was the twenty-two children who ultimately landed safely in Fort Lauderdale and in the arms of their waiting parents.

She realized then it was not time for her to break away from Haiti. "Normal life" would have to wait. Kathi decided to search for a reputable, financially stable organization in Haiti that she could partner with long-term not only to improve the quality of life for orphaned children but also to empower women, one village at a time.

From March to September 2010, Kathi spent a week and a half per month in Haiti working with five different enterprises. She decided to partner with a Haitian nonprofit run by Pastor Renelus Maxime. Craig met Pastor Maxime while filming *Stuck* in rural Haiti. He told Kathi the pastor operated a church, school, and orphanage in the small mountain village of Kenscoff. Following the earthquake, sixty orphans were living in tents on the side of the mountain.

Chances for Children began a partnership with the pastor's organization, and between December 2010 and 2012, construction projects included new schools, churches, a medical clinic, and several crèches. She made sure to supply the children with toys and games that would encourage them to solve problems and use their imaginations. Years earlier, when she was first raising her three kids, Kathi was sitting with Quinn in the middle of living room chairs that she'd set up to look like airplane rows. Toys served as passengers. She began showing Quinn how to spread his arms out like wings.

"I was watching Amelec and Espie looking out the doors of their bedrooms like, *What are they doing?*" she recalls. "Not asking to play, but watching; they were captivated."

The women of Haiti were another important focus for Kathi and Pastor Maxime. They built a community center in Kenscoff where women learn how to earn money and their independence, and consequently, keep their children.

"Sometimes we can be very judgmental about these birth mothers because they have five and six kids," Kathi says. "Why don't they use birth control? But what I've come to learn is that these mothers love their children. They are great moms. They just find themselves in situations where they're desperate. They're desperate for a man to take care of them so that's why they get pregnant again. There are so many factors, but the love that they have for their kids really is incredible. They'll do anything for them. It breaks my heart that they have to make this very difficult decision, not because they don't love their child, but because they have no hope to take care of the child. It's tough to watch."

How different Kathi and Craig's life together looked in 2013. Just seven years earlier they had been a team of two, best friends who did everything together. Now they had three thriving children, two charitable foundations, and in August 2013, nearly three thousand miles between them. Kathi decided to spend ten months in Haiti to train and mentor the future leaders of the Kenscoff community. She brought along Espie, twelve, and enrolled her in a private Christian school for the duration of their trip. Kathi says the time together strengthened their relationship, and although Espie doesn't remember her life in Haiti, her daughter got the chance to feel the satisfaction of serving others who need help.

"Espie was great with the kids," Kathi says. "She really enjoyed taking care of the toddlers. Every Saturday night we had two or three kids over from the orphanage for movie night, and she really took pride in that. The kids waited in line for movie night."

Craig and Kathi are busy at home in Scottsdale managing their foundations and caring for thirteen-year-old Amelec (who loves all sports), twelve-year-old Espie (who loves fashion design), and eight-year-old Quinn (who loves performing in school plays). Their bond is strong, as is the sentiment that family ties are for life.

"I talk about it now with the boys," Craig explains. "I say, 'When you get older, you're going to take me out to dinner,' or 'I'll come for a visit and we'll have Sunday dinner at your house.' We talk about it in the context of family and being connected forever but that the roles might change. I'm teaching Amelec to barbecue, and we were barbecuing the other night and I said, 'Y'know, there's going to come a time, son, when you're going to have your wife and your kids and your family, and we're going to show up and you're going to have to barbecue for us, so you better get pretty good at this soon.' He loved that."

Kathi will continue indefinitely to commute to Haiti for a brief stay every six weeks, growing and maintaining the many facets of her foundation. The Juntunens

Kathi in Port-au-Prince, 2013 *(Courtesy of Kathi Juntunen)*

acknowledge that the time they spend apart and that Kathi spends away from the kids may appear unconventional to many couples. But they feel strongly that while their three kids are the hands-down priority, they also feel compelled to speak for millions of voiceless children around the globe.

"We are both consumed by the sense of responsibility to serve kids we feel are neglected," Craig says, "and that sense of responsibility and the passion to change things for these kids has trumped the traditional confines of a marriage. Our marriage now looks different from lots of other marriages because we're living apart periodically. I think we're both focused and energized about trying to achieve something that has a much broader impact than just worrying about taking care of 'us.' There was an enormous sacrifice to what Kathi was doing when she spent ten months in Haiti. It wasn't just being away from the person she married seventeen years earlier: she was away from her two boys, the comforts of the lifestyle she knew, her family and friends; she was away from a lot of things that brought her comfort. She was living in a very harsh, demanding, frustrating environment. It would be very, very easy for just the general living conditions to wear her down to the point where she says, 'I've had enough; I'm coming home for good.' But that's not Kath."

Kathi's days in Haiti were and are long indeed. She

might leave the community at four forty-five a.m. to drive
a sick baby to the hospital and not return until ten p.m.
There are meetings with birth moms in the community or
social welfare officials in town. Groups from the States who
fly in to help need direction and supplies for their projects.

"It's not like you can just go to Home Depot. I'll go to
six different hardware stores to find all the things I need,"
she explains, "and each hardware store takes about an hour
because the process is so messed up. You always wait in
Haiti. It's a country with no infrastructure, a lot of graft
and corruption."

Haiti's electricity is intermittent, its poverty constant.
Daily, Kathi is approached by desperate people in need of
money whom she has to deny; donations must fund projects that will effect lasting change. The Juntunens' new path
is anything but easy, they both admit.

"As hard as it is, as hard as it is to be away from Craig
and the kids, I don't question it; I don't have any doubts
about it. This work is what I'm supposed to be doing. I have
a calm about me; a peace. Now . . . some days I want to
quit," she says, laughing. "Don't get me wrong . . ."

Craig admits, "Doing what we're trying to do is very,
very hard—surprisingly hard. There are days I feel like
quitting, but how could I quit and not feel like a coward? I
know there is a solution out there for these kids. I can't tell

you how many times I run into people and they say they read my book, or they saw *Stuck*, or they wanted to adopt but got discouraged. So, as I've gone down this path, I have so much information—and that's the cursed part, because if I was to walk away from it, I would feel that I was a coward and I didn't do something that I should be doing."

Craig is now fifty-nine, Kathi fifty-six. Late in life, the Never Dad and his very accomplished wife went from realizing their dream together to living a life they never imagined in their wildest dreams.

"Our kids are such a cornerstone of our being now," Craig says, "and that all came because we considered, we jumped in, and now we're doing it. As humans, I think we have a tendency to hunker down within our comfort zone, and at times our heart tells us to cross that line and to be bold, but our mind tells us to play it safe—that if we venture out into the unknown there could be this enormous dose of pain, so we stay with what we know and is easy for us. But sometimes that doesn't produce the most meaningful life experience, and that was a lesson that we really learned. We thought we were comfortable, but taking this risk put us into such a different place, which has opened up so many opportunities to learn and grow and evolve as humans. It's given our life a much different dimension than had we just stayed playing golf every day and living in our own little bubble. Life would not have been nearly as meaningful as it is today."

For more information on both foundations:

Chances4Children.org
BothEndsBurning.org

(Courtesy of Mark Burnett and Roma Downey)

knew that God would send an angel for my baby, and here you are.'"

Roma said a prayer with the mother and left the hospital, conflicted and concerned. When she got home, she immediately called her *Touched* castmate and dear friend Della Reese. Through tears, Roma expressed her anxiety that she might appear to be something that she wasn't. Della reached out from the other end of the phone.

"She said, 'Baby, she didn't need an actress; she needed an angel.' And I said, 'But she thought that God had sent me there.' Della answered, 'Who said he didn't?'"

God and faith were a significant part of Roma's personal life well before her professional career. She grew up Roman Catholic in Northern Ireland and went to church every day. At ten years old, Roma lost her mother to a heart attack. She says her father's strong faith provided their heartbroken family the comfort and courage to move forward. Her own strong faith consoled her at twenty when her father died.

Roma went on to study art and drama, and found work on Broadway and television. She would marry and divorce—and give birth to a daughter—before she crossed paths with Mark Burnett.

"My feet were in a bucket of water," she says, laughing. In 2004, Roma was getting a manicure and pedicure at the same salon where Mark was getting his hair cut. Their eyes met in the mirror several times, and both separately asked the receptionist, "Who is that?"

Mark was the prolific and successful television producer of megahit series such as *Survivor* and *Celebrity Apprentice*. A father of two sons, he'd divorced a year earlier. Mark was also raised in the United Kingdom, in London, where his Scottish parents had moved for more religious freedom and economic opportunity. His father was Catholic, his mother Protestant.

"There was less of a religious divide in London, a more cosmopolitan city," Mark explains. "In Scotland, Catholics couldn't even get jobs."

When Roma and Mark began dating, they discovered they shared blue-collar backgrounds, raising children, and a belief in God. But Roma led with her faith; Mark tucked his in with a variety of other convictions he valued in life. That would change. But in Mark's case, there was no pit in his stomach or voice in his head that told him something was missing, that he wasn't where he belonged in terms of quality of life. The change for Mark was gradual. Call it divine intervention. An "angel" was placed in his life.

"In retrospect, you look at it and realize Roma was facilitating the change in her loving way all along," Mark says, "but not in a pushy way at all; it's not Roma's style.

She's got kind of a cool vibe and doesn't try to tell anybody what to do. She stayed in loving space all the time. But, no question; it's a God's-plan thing."

The two married in April 2007. That same year, Roma approached Mark about bringing the story of the Bible to television in an epic and intimate way. The couple had watched Cecil B. DeMille's 1956 version of *The Ten Commandments* with their teenagers, who commented on what they felt were dated graphics and a hokey representation of the story. Mark agreed with Roma that there was an opportunity to create an updated series that would appeal to all age groups and portray the Bible as God's love story to us, not a rule book. They began to reach out to top-tier artists in areas like special effects and musical scoring. Forty biblical scholars were brought in to verify the accuracy of the script. Faith leaders consulted on set. Roma played the role of Mother Mary. The series would cover Genesis to Revelation with five two-hour segments on the History channel.

"The minute we took it out into the world," Roma says, "there was great resistance initially—that we had lost our minds. There were certain people advising us that we would lose our shirts and our reputations, that we would look foolish. But at that point we were unstoppable."

And audiences couldn't stop watching. When *The Bible*

On the set of *The Bible*, Morocco, 2012 *(Photograph by Joe Alblas/© 2012 LightWorkers Media, LLC. All rights reserved.)*

aired March 3–31, 2013, it garnered cable television ratings not seen before. Following several subsequent airings, the miniseries received more than one hundred million cumulative views. But those are just numbers.

While Roma was extremely fulfilled to have spread God's message of love to so many, she was also gratified to watch the effect that five years of daily immersion in the Bible had on Mark.

"It's been beautiful to see how his heart has just bloomed in the grace of the Lord," she says. "There's just more of him. He's more available to the range of his own emotions and consequently he's deeper in connection with God and therefore with everyone."

As executive producer of blockbuster network television series including *The Voice* and *Shark Tank*, Mark understands how programs move and inspire viewers. But this time, *The Bible* not only inspired countless others, it changed him and his image of God.

"Once you accept Jesus, he's not going to be taken away from you. He could be disappointed in you, but he's not going to leave you," he says. "Once you've taken the Hand, you're in for the long haul."

In 2013, Roma and Mark produced *Son of God*, a recut (with added scenes) of *The Bible* released in theaters in 2014. Two different networks aired miniseries they produced, *The*

*Dovekeepers* and *A.D.*, a follow-up series to *The Bible*. They are working together on a remake of *Ben Hur*, for release in theaters in 2016.

"It's a shift, and it's a shift that's for the long term," Mark says of his deepened faith. "What are we going to do with it going forward? Not sure. Maybe our contribution to spreading the light is through media. Maybe we are bridge builders in Hollywood across faith communities. Maybe that's our path."

And maybe God does send us angels.

Having a place to go—is a home.

Having someone to love—is a family.

Having both—is a blessing.

—DONNA HEDGES

## ➤➤ NESHAMA ABRAHAM ◄◄
## AND ZEV PAISS

There is a small, remote kingdom called Bhutan in South Asia set on the slopes of the Eastern Himalayas. Forty years ago, a former king proposed an interesting idea: let's determine the success of our country by measuring the well-being of our citizens, *not* our economy. His idea became an index known as "gross national happiness," to counter the existing gross domestic product index. The GNH gauged the country's success by asking people about their quality of life, their relationship with the environment, how well they were being governed, and their sense of belonging to their culture. Today, Bhutan is not without problems, but the happiness level of its citizens continues to play a role in how the country moves forward.

On a one-acre plot of land in Boulder, Colorado, residents have set the bar high for their GNH index: gross neighborhood happiness.

During the 1920s, a private mansion served as the prize at the end of a long driveway in the exclusive neighborhood of Old Westbury on Long Island's North Shore. A family who made millions mining copper built the lavish home and named it the Columns. A total of ten white pillars supported both a second-story porch and the presumption by visitors that those who lived inside were extremely moneyed.

When Amelia Lobsenz and Dr. Harry Abrahams bought the Columns in 1961, it was her money that funded the purchase—money earned mining clients, not copper. Five years earlier, Amelia had started her own public relations firm, Lobsenz PR, a pioneering move by a thirty-four-year-old woman in a male-dominated industry. A gutsy businesswoman and gifted writer, Amelia founded her company on powerhouse clients including the Rockefeller brothers and Nestlé. When they moved into the Columns, Amelia and Harry, a surgeon, brought with them their blended family: Michael, Amelia's eleven-year-old son from a first marriage; George, Harry's ten-year-old son from his first marriage; and one-year-old Kay, their

The Columns, Old Westbury, New York *(Courtesy of Neshama Abraham)*

baby daughter. Because she was so much younger than her half brothers, Kay essentially grew up as an only child in a four-story estate.

"To give you an idea of how big this house was," she says, "there was an entire large room dedicated to my Barbie collection. There were houses for all the dolls, their own mini mansions. It was really quite elaborate."

The Columns stood as the stately centerpiece of ten lush acres. Upper and lower gardens bloomed throughout the year, their vivid beauty enhanced by the soothing sound of babbling formal fountains. Travelers along the lengthy, winding driveway gazed across a vast lawn featuring a triangle of copper beech trees that flashed their showy hue each autumn. The property had ample room for an Olympic-sized pool, an innovative Har-Tru tennis court, and a stable occupied by a pony named Clover, a gift to Dr. Abrahams from a grateful patient.

"My dad saved the life of a man who owned harness-race horses at the Roosevelt Raceway," Kay recalls. "It was a very complicated operation so he gave us a beagle and a Shetland pony as an additional thank-you."

The mansion's interior measured ten thousand square feet, liberally apportioned into twenty-five rooms.

The marble floor in the formal entryway led to four levels of seemingly endless spaces, each with its own

Formal entrance, the Columns *(Courtesy of Neshama Abraham)*

generous porch. Elegances from the original owners remained, like hand-painted wallpaper imported from France by the famous American interior designer Lady Mendl, whose wealthy clients in the early 1900s ranged from the Duke and Duchess of Windsor to Anne Vander- bilt. Chandeliers, also brought in from Europe by Lady Mendl, hung from high ceilings throughout the house. Off the kitchen and main dining area was a sunny break- fast room decorated with blue leather seats and large mirrors featuring the French technique of *verre églomisé*, a reverse painting on the mirror's glass; in this case, the artist depicted a woman's dressing room complete with masks from a masquerade ball and chests of drawers overflowing with pearls and jewels. Four to six servants were on duty full-time to manage the massive home and property.

What the house was missing, quite often, were the owners. Kay's dad worked long hours serving as chief of surgery at a large Long Island hospital and also as the Nassau County medical examiner. Her mom was also ex- tremely busy as chief executive officer of the successful and growing public relations firm she founded and ran.

"As a little kid I felt neglected and lonely," says Kay. "My mom was so successful, so busy, so driven. She'd come home exhausted; she had very little left to give to a young daughter. We always had dinner together at seven o'clock. A chauffeur would drive her home from her office in Manhattan to Long Island and she'd be working in the back with the partition closed most of the time. My dad was handy and made a beautiful wooden desk for the back of the sky-blue limousine. She had a Dictaphone and a typewriter. My grandmother knitted her warm afghan blankets that she'd wrap around herself during drives to and from Manhattan on cold days."

Kay treasured the nights when her mother had enough energy left to spin stories for her about a chipmunk Amelia called Chippy. Quality time with her mother always ended too soon.

"We had this one closet off the formal entrance that was dedicated primarily to my mom's fur coats. When she left in the morning, I would take all the coats off their hangers and lay them down to create a furry little cave. I would lie down and smell them because they smelled like her perfume," she says. "It might sound strange, but cuddling with her furs was one of the only ways I could feel close to her because she was gone so much."

Older by nine and ten years, George and Michael were not ideal playmates for Kay. Plus, very large properties put great distance between neighbors in Old Westbury; no one stopped by or played in the street. Kay further isolated

herself, too self-conscious about the family's wealth to in-
vite over friends from school. Even hide-and-seek, typi-
cally enjoyable, was for Kay a confirmation that she was
invisible, a ghost hiding but not missed behind heavy formal curtains.

"When my parents were around and I decided to
hide, I thought, *Is anyone going to notice?* The problem
was that my mom was so work focused; she just wasn't
mother oriented. She had people dedicated to keeping
the house clean, and taking care of the gardens, the laundry and cooking, and the cars—all the tasks of running
the estate—but there wasn't a nanny. There wasn't a person to take care of me or watch out for me when I came
home from school. My mother just didn't think I needed
a caretaker, even though the formal gardens did. I guess
she assumed with all these people around I'd be fine, but
they were focused on the household tasks, not a child who
needed attention."

Kay's maternal grandmother, Florence, visited several
days a week. She taught her granddaughter about the Ten
Commandments, and together they colored, cut out paper
dolls, and worked on needlepoint. Her beloved Grandma
Freitag was one of the only people who entered into the
bubble of loneliness and entitlement that was Kay's life.

When he was seventeen, her oldest half brother warned Kay about the pitfalls of privilege.

"Right before he left for college, Michael and I had a heart-to-heart talk. He said, 'Kay, you are becoming a JAP [Jewish American Princess]. You're getting really spoiled.' He painted a picture of who I could become if I kept on that path. I was only seven but I got it. I said, 'Okay. Thank you.' I made a mental decision that I was not going to be obnoxious, spoiled, haughty, or demanding. I am very critical and demanding, but primarily of myself. I'm a perfectionist in many areas, but I wasn't going to be spoiled or materialistic. I didn't choose that path, even though there was plenty of wealth."

Any free time for the family was filled with weekend ski trips to Vermont's Bromley Mountain and the private Windham Mountain Club in the northern Catskills. Kay became an accomplished skier and also tapped into her parents' love of tennis. Their pristine home court featured a special soft surface, and the sport became a way for Kay and her dad to spend time together.

"I would often get up with him very early—even in pajamas sometimes—and we'd play tennis before he'd go to the hospital."

She also joined in the Thursday afternoon "doctors'

game" of tennis that her father hosted for fellow physicians. By the time she was twelve, Kay was training at the prestigious Port Washington Tennis Academy in Long Island with the likes of John McEnroe and Mary Carillo.

"Whenever I'd see Mary she'd say, 'Hey, Kay, what do you say?' She has a great sense of humor. John didn't have the best tennis etiquette. He'd throw his racquet, and you'd see it sailing through the air and then landing one inch from your head. That's who he was back then."

Kay was so skilled by the time she entered high school in 1974 that she opted out of the girls' tennis team and played on the more competitive boys' team for four years, serving in her senior year as team captain. She also traveled to Europe during high school to play in competitive tennis tournaments hosted by the US State Department.

When it came time to choose a college, Kay says she and her parents focused on academics and never considered that she would continue playing tennis. But following an interview in the admissions office at Rice University, Kay decided to walk over to the tennis courts. She had a chance meeting with the men's tennis coach, and when Kay told him she held a top-ten ranking in the United States Tennis Association Eastern Section, he asked her if she'd consider a full tennis scholarship to Rice. Title IX legislation that offered increased athletic opportunities for women prompted universities like Rice to reexamine their athletics programs. The men's coach told Kay they were hiring a new women's coach and that she could be the team's number one player and provide a solid foundation for the building of a competitive program. Kay accepted the offer.

In August 1978, she was off to Rice University in Houston, her first foray into the world beyond her worry-free childhood. Reality hit even before she left home.

"It was the night before college and I had never done my own laundry. I realized, *Oh my gosh! How the heck am I going to manage?*"

She asked the housekeeper who handled the laundry for guidance.

"That night, I did my first load of laundry; she showed me how to sew on a button, how to repair a basic tear. I didn't know how to cook anything either. It was so embarrassing; I didn't know how to boil an egg, I didn't even know how to make oatmeal," she admits. "I could put cereal in a bowl and pour milk on it and I could make toast, but that was about it."

College for Kay was invigorating and, as a student athlete, extremely busy. The mental and physical demands were constant.

"When I took finals at Rice, a lot of them I took on the road in a hotel room. I would say to my teammates,

'I'm going to be doing my sociology final starting now, so please don't bother me for two hours.' I'd sign the honor code at the beginning: *Here's when I started. Here's when I ended. I have neither given nor received aid on this exam.* That's what you do as an athlete. You're very visible, too. Everyone watches your matches. There was pressure as the number one player. I felt responsible to help Rice build a team, so I needed to win my matches so we could recruit even better players for our team."

But why work so hard? Kay could have simply lounged in the hammock of her financial net. Instead, she pushed herself, driven by the feeling that she wasn't good enough in her parents' eyes. Kay says her mom and dad didn't openly acknowledge that they were proud of her, so she overachieved in an effort to "earn" her parents' love and respect.

"My mother was so high achieving, and I think she felt that's just who you are in the world; there's nothing less than excellence and you must give your all," Kay explains. "She worked all the time, including while she sat by the pool on weekends. She taught me the value of being productive, to fill your time by always getting things done. Her thought was, *What's a life worth living unless you do your best?*"

At Rice, Kay was studying philosophy but, since age

fourteen, had been interning in the field she saw as her career: public relations. Amelia had introduced Kay to a colleague, which led to an unpaid summer position at Colgate-Palmolive during high school. She learned to write speeches for the head of corporate communications and articles for the company newsletter. In college, Kay interned for two global communications firms.

"My mom was willing to help open a door, but it was very clear I was the one who had to walk through and do the work."

During Kay's sophomore year, the family experienced a scary and heartbreaking event. Harry suffered a series of mini strokes that led him to retire early as a doctor and surgeon.

"It was devastating for Dad and sad for me. He didn't know what to do with his time," Kay explains. "He went from being highly active to sitting around watching TV. He gained weight and became sluggish mentally and physically. He hadn't planned for retirement and Mom was too busy to see what was happening."

Now the sole provider, Amelia moved quickly to sell the Columns, their home for two decades. They downsized to an elegant home in the upscale village of Old Brookville.

In January 1983, Kay graduated from Rice. She could

have joined Lobsenz-Stevens Incorporated (Amelia took on a partner in 1975), but she knew: not yet.

"I didn't want to begin my career as the CEO's daughter. I doubt if I would have been respected. I didn't even know if I'd learn well. I needed to start at the bottom, develop my skills like everyone else, and work my way up." As much as Amelia would have loved to have her daughter beside her, "she was a consummate professional and knew it was the right thing for me to do."

Kay moved immediately to New York City for a job on Madison Avenue with Carl Byoir and Associates, the third-largest PR firm in the world. Amelia's name got her noticed, but Kay had to apply for the job, go through an interview, and prove her skills on writing tests. She had a lot to prove as Amelia's daughter, a woman, and a new college graduate in a firm full of older, experienced newspaper journalists.

Over the next three years, Kay worked sixteen-hour days, juggling ten clients. Her personal relationship with a young attorney working a similarly demanding schedule lasted a year.

"We'd come home—totally spent zombies—sit down, order Chinese food, and watch *Star Trek*."

During this frenetic time in Kay's life, in 1987, the family faced a second devastating medical development:

sixty-five-year-old Amelia was diagnosed with breast cancer.

"I wasn't involved in her chemo or radiation treatments," Kay recalls. "She didn't talk about what she was going through and did not once ask for help. She was so independent."

Thankfully, the treatments were effective and Amelia survived.

Kay worked for two well-respected Manhattan PR firms before joining her mother at Lobsenz-Stevens in 1989. The firm was thriving with a wide range of solid accounts, including banks, car manufacturers, pharmaceutical companies, and overseas countries; annual billings were in the tens of millions of dollars. Kay was well respected and was promoted quickly from managing accounts to acquiring new clients. She and her mom had dinner weekly and became closer as they shared time and work matters.

Sadly, in 1991, within two years of Kay's joining the company, Amelia suffered a recurrence of cancer; it resurfaced in her spine. The prognosis was poor and she told Kay that she wanted the news kept quiet at work.

"She got so weak that she couldn't even open the door to the New York office on Park Avenue," says Kay. "She didn't want anyone to know, so in the mornings I would meet her at the front door and open it for her to walk in."

After her diagnosis, Amelia wanted to sell her thirty-five-year-old firm to give the family a financial cushion but couldn't find the right buyer.

By late 1991, Amelia was enduring severe pain in her spine and was hospitalized in Lenox Hill Hospital, several blocks from Kay's apartment on the Upper East Side. Kay's father in recent years had experienced additional small strokes and spoke little. At thirty-one, Kay was about to enter the most challenging period of her life.

"I would go to work, check on my mom at Lenox Hill Hospital during lunch, go back to work, and then I would take the Long Island Rail Road home to make sure Dad was okay at the house in Old Brookville, where he had round-the-clock care," she recalls. "I did that virtually every day for a year. It was sad and exhausting."

Kay had little support. Her half brothers lived out of state. Home healthcare workers kept the Old Brookville home clean and cooked for her father. Working long hours compounded by the grief of watching her mother die and father decline completely drained Kay.

"One day I was walking in the hall that connected my mother's apartment building and my building, and I remember just stopping and sobbing. I realized how incredibly exhausted I was and how I had completely given up my personal life. Like many kids of aging parents, my life was solely focused on work and taking care of my parents."

On September 1, 1992, Amelia died. Kay was with her and received an unexpected gift from her seventy-year-old mother.

"A mom who is so hardworking and who was a perfectionist is critical by nature. It wasn't until she was literally on her deathbed when I actually felt that she complimented me without a backhanded, 'And you should do this now.' A typical compliment from my mom was, 'Oh, that's a really nice outfit but you really need to use more makeup.' But on the day before she died she simply said, 'You're doing wonderfully.' It didn't have anything attached to it or a recommendation for improvement. I needed that parting gift to feel that she loved me purely for who I was."

Amelia had asked the family not to let the world know she was gravely ill. But a few days before passing away, she agreed to let Kay send notices to colleagues around the world sharing the unfortunate news of Amelia's losing battle with cancer. Kay felt it was imperative to give the people who knew and admired Amelia a chance to send their love. Her amazing mother had broken new ground in the industry, was the first female president of the International Public Relations Association, and maintained relationships around the globe.

"The first bag of letters and telegrams and correspondence arrived the day *after* she died," Kay says with sadness. "She didn't get to know how much she mattered to people. It would have meant so much to her to hear how many people considered her a role model. How she broke through the glass ceiling and laid a path for other women to achieve at high levels in public relations. I sat by myself and read the letters out loud as I would have done for my mom if she were still alive."

Amelia's death took a toll on Harry, her husband of nearly thirty-five years. Kay watched her father essentially give up on living.

"He was in hospice; he was checking out. Mom had died, so what reason did he think he had to live? At one point he stopped eating, and I just said, 'Dad, I'm here for you. Don't die. Please don't go. I can't lose you and Mom at the same time.'"

Kay moved her father into what had been her mother's nearby New York apartment and began the process of loving him back to life. At the same time she was tackling the mountain of paperwork that was her parents' estate. There was also the sorting and selling of countless possessions from the Old Brookville house and additional properties. It was clear to Kay that the next few years would require focus and energy that could not be sustained while working at Lobsenz-Stevens. In 1993, she sold her shares of stock in the company.

"I felt that I have one father and he has to be more important than anything else at this point," she explains. "When you look back at your life, it's really who you loved and who loved you, and how you spent your time with those you're close with. It's not going to be how much money you made or how much real estate property you owned or possessions. Love is the value that matters most at the end of your life."

Kay hired music and art therapists to help engage her father emotionally so he could process his grief from losing Amelia. She spent time with him sitting and talking, or pushing him in his wheelchair during neighborhood strolls through the Upper East Side of Manhattan.

Kay also began the process of healing herself. Completely spent from the stress of the last few years, she took up yoga and soon after became a certified instructor. She then created a unique form of yoga that incorporated Judaism and led classes several times a week in Upper West Side synagogues. Faith provided comfort for Kay, and she became active in the local Jewish Renewal community. She volunteered as executive director for the P'nai Or of Manhattan and took turns with other members holding home-based Shabbat services.

As the next few years passed and matters of the estate lessened, Kay began to consider starting her own public relations company. In 1995, she founded Abraham and Associates. Her first client proved to be nearly eighteen hundred miles away in Colorado. Kay had flown from New York City to Fort Collins to participate in a Jewish Renewal conference. At the event, she met the chief executive officer of a Boulder-based company called Career Track, and he agreed to sign on with her new company.

In the months ahead, Kay flew back so often to Boulder that she rented a room in a house to stay in during her work trips. She loved the city's reverence for and easy access to nature and its residents' commitment to health and wellness.

"I would walk outside during the middle of the day and people would be jogging on trails and biking, and I thought, *Oh my gosh—you're allowed to do this; you're allowed to take time off to exercise and experience nature.* No one looks at you like, *Why aren't you working right now?*"

The more she experienced the juxtaposition between the hiking trails in Boulder and the cement and skyscrapers of New York, the more she wondered whether a move west could reconnect her with her once active, healthy self. During one of her stays in Boulder, she walked to a nearby park next to a lake called Wonderland.

"I was sitting on the swings facing the mountains and I had this epiphany. I heard my inner voice: *You could live here. You don't have to keep doing this commute. When you have children they could swing here, too, and grow up in Boulder and see the lake, and be connected to the mountains and nature.*"

In early 1996, thirty-six-year-old Kay decided to rent her New York apartment and experience what life would be like in Boulder. Kay's to-do list for relocating was long and included getting a mammogram. In April, she went to her scheduled appointment. Following the procedure, the radiologist looked over the X-ray and requested one more. After the second X-ray, the radiologist asked for another.

"After the third one she said, 'Look, this is exactly what cancer looks like. I'm sorry to tell you that you have breast cancer.'"

The same horrible words that were told to her mother.

But, fortunately, Kay's cancer had not spread to her lymph nodes or bloodstream. Doctors explained to Kay that with her form of medium-grade breast cancer, radiation would lessen the chance of recurrence by 5 percent. She elected to undergo surgery but not radiation.

The already-scheduled movers arrived the day after Kay's diagnosis to take her belongings to Colorado. Friends in Boulder kindly agreed to meet and unload the truck whenever it arrived.

Kay delayed leaving until June so she could have surgery and recover. Breast cancer scared both her and her father, but it also confirmed Kay's decision to move them to a more peaceful, healing environment.

Once in Boulder, Kay rented town homes for herself and her dad in the same complex. She hired round-the-clock care for him and enlisted the help of a naturopathic physician to rejuvenate her body with herbs and other holistic treatments. Having visited often before the move, Kay had developed friendships within the Jewish Renewal Community of Boulder, a sister community to the group in New York where she served as executive director.

In August, two months after her move, Kay participated in a community event called the Dances of Universal Peace, where participants sing and enjoy dances from around the world. She arrived late to the event because she had been on a dinner date.

"I got this inner message of sorts that I needed to go to the dances."

As was etiquette, when the last dance ended, people stood in silence and hugged those near them. Kay noticed a man whose name was Zev Paiss.

"He had a much-too-short haircut and a very warm smile," Kay recalls.

Zev and Kay hugged with no words spoken.

"He was polite and had the right balance of *I noticed you . . . I'm interested in you . . . but this is as far as we can go in this setting since we're silent*. But," she says, "a spark was lit."

One month later, a group from the Jewish Renewal Community gathered for a trip to Idaho Springs, where caves provided spring water for a ritual cleanse before Rosh Hashanah. Kay rode with friends; Zev rode with his dear friend Miriam, who had met Kay and liked her. During the thirty-five-minute ride, Zev asked Miriam questions about the new woman from New York City.

"She was obviously Jewish," Zev says, "and I thought she was adorable, very attractive. She was a couple of inches shorter than me. She seemed very smart and articulate"— he laughs—"and she was single."

Zev and Kay soaked in separate caves, and afterward, all the men and women sat down together to have an open conversation about the experience and to share their insights on faith.

The third meeting between Kay and Zev was not by chance. In October, several weeks after Idaho Springs, Zev made it a point to attend an event he was sure Kay would go to as well—the Simchat Torah celebration, a reenactment of Moses receiving the Torah from God. Everyone took turns dancing with the Torah and passing it on to the next person.

"At the end of my turn dancing with the Torah," Kay says, "he came over and said, 'Can we have tea?' and I answered, 'Well, how about dinner?'"

Zev was pleased. "I thought, *Okay, well this is a really good sign.*"

So, how *would* the two get along? Zev's middle-class upbringing was completely different from Kay's cushy seat in the lap of luxury. He grew up in a 2,500-square-foot house that he moved into with his mother at eight years old when his parents divorced. The home in Woodland Hills, in the San Fernando Valley region of Los Angeles, was fifteen minutes from where his father lived. He had a close relationship with his mom and spent weekends at his dad's house babysitting his younger sister and brother while his father took a date to dinner or a movie. After high school, Zev worked his way through college as a chef and majored in marine biology at the University of California, Santa Barbara. In his junior year, Zev transferred to Oakes College at UC Santa Cruz to participate in a special program focused on marine mammals. An exciting part of the program involved studying a colony of seals that lived on a small island off the California coast.

"It was sort of my Jacques Cousteau experience," he says with a laugh. "For an entire winter on Friday mornings I would don a wetsuit and get into a little inflatable boat and ride a quarter mile out to the island with a few other students. We kept track of the elephant seals, monitoring, weighing, and marking them."

But it was a class on land that changed the direction of Zev's life. A course titled "Utopian Visions of a Modern World" exposed him to the idea of using environmental and economic strategies to create sustainable communities. He studied the various ways that responsible planning could lead to long-term prosperity.

"That's what really opened me up to the fact that we can save the dolphins and the whales," says Zev, "but if we as humans don't figure out better ways of doing things, it's not really going to matter."

In June 1980, Zev graduated with degrees in environmental planning and aquatic biology. He spent the summer in Oregon working as a planning intern at an "intentional community" that was under development. Over the next few years, he learned about alternative wastewater treatment and solar design, and also cooked in restaurants and worked on construction sites.

In 1985, Zev moved to Boulder and got married. Just five years later, his life would change in two significant ways: he went through a divorce, and he attended the first International Ecocity Conference in Berkeley, held to discuss how best to reform cities to be in balance with nature.

During the 1990 conference, the founders of a movement called cohousing spoke and explained the strategies featured in their book, *Cohousing: A Contemporary Approach to Housing Ourselves*.

"I came back from the conference to Boulder," Zev says, "and immediately went to the bookstore and read the cohousing book and thought, *Oh, okay. This makes sense; this is the next step for me*."

Within two years, he boarded a plane to Denmark, the birthplace of cohousing, or what the Danes call "living community," made popular in the 1970s.

"Their situation was very similar to ours. They had a growing middle class, there were a lot of people with full-time jobs who ended up with latchkey kids who didn't have anybody there when they got home," Zev explains. "They said, 'There's got to be a better way to organize our neighborhoods to deal with the realities of our lives.'"

The concept was brought back to the United States in the early 1980s by two American architects doing their graduate studies in Denmark. Instead of using the Danish term "living community," they labeled the neighborhood model "cohousing." Following his trip to Denmark, Zev created a slide show and traveled the western United States educating people about cohousing.

In 1992, he rented a home in Nyland Cohousing, a

large rural cohousing community outside Denver. With 135 residents living in 42 homes, the development on 140 acres was too large and relied too heavily on cars for Zev's liking, but he wanted to get a feel for the experience. In the meantime, he and a group of future residents were searching for an ideal parcel of land where they could develop a smaller, more urban cohousing community in Boulder.

In 1993, Zev took a second trip to Denmark and, over the next two years, created a video presentation to replace the slide show. He continued consulting and training groups on how to form, design, and develop cohousing communities. At that time, only seven neighborhoods were up and running in the United States, primarily in California, Colorado, and Washington State.

In 1996, Zev was four years into renting at the large cohousing community and preparing to make a move. He and his future cohabitants had located a one-acre piece of land in an urban setting that would accommodate eleven homes. They named the community Nomad after the adjacent Nomad Theater, which sold them the land. Zev reserved a 675-square-foot one-bedroom home with an unfinished basement.

And that brings us back to the summer of 1996, when two sets of eyes met across the dance floor.

From Zev's journal:

*It was a good time for me to reconnect with the group and
many people were there. One very new one and someone
who has caught my eye the first time I saw her is Kay. I
wonder what her Hebrew name is? I will have to ask. She
is a beautiful pixie of a woman and very feminine and
dances nice and is single, Jewish, intelligent, very beautiful,
and lives right here in Boulder.*

On their first date—dinner at an Indian restaurant—
Zev asked Kay about her Hebrew name. She was amazed
because she'd been silently using a Hebrew name during
meditation. The name signified the deep breath taken
when the soul enters and leaves the body.

"When he asked me, I decided to verbalize it. I said,
'Well, the name that I like is Neshama.' He said, 'Can I call
you that?'"

From that night on, Kay became Neshama. She and
Zev had made a deep connection during their first three
encounters and over a long dinner.

"We covered an amazing amount of territory," Zev
recalls. "It was obvious that neither of us were kidding
around. We both wanted to know what the other person
was about. We talked about religion and spirituality, and

children. By the end of that evening it was clear that there was something very powerful here already, and that was our first date."

Zev invited Neshama to an event that weekend he was hosting. Leaders in the cohousing movement from across the country were gathering to discuss the latest challenges and advancements. Zev had told Neshama over dinner about his passion for sustainable communities, but she had a lot to learn.

"The word 'sustainability,'" she says, "was not even a part of my vocabulary at that point."

Neshama was falling in love with a man whose vision of "community" was very different from hers.

"That second date made it clear to me: *Hmm . . . this is something Zev is really passionate about. He's going to want to live in one.*"

By December, just four months after they met, the two were pressed to determine the depth of their love.

"When I met Neshama," Zev explains, "we had to quickly decide whether this was real for us, and if so, we had to switch homes because the home I had reserved was not going to work for the two of us, especially if we were going to have children."

Neshama agreed to take a leap of faith, with a caveat.

"My agreement with Zev was: I'll try cohousing for

two years, but if it's not working, I reserve the right to move out of the community and into the house that I originally thought I would move into. That house would be much more isolated, up in the woods, where I could walk out and not see anyone. It would be very different from this style of living where I would be next to more than two dozen people on one acre of land."

"I was open to that," Zev says. "I didn't know how it was going to work for me, either, being in the industry as well as being a resident. Certainly our commitment to each other was strong enough that I said I'm willing to try it out and we can touch base in two years."

Neshama and Zev put a contract down on one of the largest homes in the development: 2,100 square feet with a finished basement. The plan was for her father to move into the small home Zev had reserved before they met. In Neshama's mind, adding custom touches to the existing blueprints would help ease the transition into such a new and different living experience.

"When we started talking about the house," Zev recalls, "she said, 'That's not going to work; I'm going to need something quite different.' I said, 'Well, I don't have the finances to be able to do that,' and at some point she said, 'I do.'"

Zev was unaware of the extent of Neshama's wealth.

She told him that *she* would finance adjustments to the house that would make it more comfortable for her: a formal entryway; additional windows; an open, winding staircase; a walk-in closet; and several of the elegant, imported chandeliers from the Columns, which were incorporated into the decor. She also wanted a home office in case they were blessed with a family.

"I felt when my kids came home, I wanted to be there. They should know that they are seen and heard and that they are loved. It's important that someone stops their work and is with you. With a successful CEO as a mother, I didn't get much one-on-one attention growing up and spent a lot of lonely time after school by myself."

Zev wanted a steam shower, a Jacuzzi-style tub, and a hot tub on the top level. Even with the upgrades, Neshama was still somewhat apprehensive.

"I remember walking through our town home when it was under construction," she says, "and the first floor was seven hundred fifty square feet, which was about the size of my New York apartment. I thought, *I moved to Colorado to live in a house—the one at the end of the long driveway, not this town home sharing walls with neighbors on either side of me.*"

Zev tried to help her envision the end result.

"I took her up to the very top floor that has this

phenomenal view of Boulder and the Flatirons. At that point she said, 'Okay, I can do this.'"

Their house would be ready in a year. The pair had collaborated so well designing the house and interacting with their neighbors in Nomad that they decided to work together. Abraham and Associates was renamed Abraham Paiss & Associates.

In June 1997, Zev accepted the role of executive director of the Cohousing Association of the United States. The couple was busy personally as well. That summer, they traveled with Harry to New York City to sell his apartment and pack up his belongings to ship to Nomad. Zev brought along an engagement ring and talked to Harry when Neshama was in the other room.

"I asked him for his blessing to marry her. He was not speaking at that point, but he smiled and nodded. I could see his eyes got wet. It was definitely a yes."

Under a full moon on the roof of Neshama's Manhattan apartment building, Zev proposed. She accepted and they were pregnant within a month. Sadly, Harry passed away in September, just two months before they were all scheduled to move into Nomad.

In November 1997, Zev and Neshama officially became cohousers. They solely owned the interior of their condominium and shared ownership of the land and the

Nomad Development, Boulder, 2010 *(Courtesy of Zev Paiss)*

exterior of the eleven total homes with their fellow cohabitants. Including Zev and Neshama, eighteen people moved into Nomad. They were all well acquainted after several years of working together to purchase the land, design the community, and oversee the construction process.

Each of their homes faced a common grassy courtyard that formed a hub, an inviting gathering place to promote daily interaction. A 750-square-foot common house was available for frequent social events—like birthday parties and community meetings—and group dinners twice a week. Teams were assigned to coordinate property workdays, stock the common house, collect homeowners' association fees, and handle other duties to keep the community running smoothly. There was also a collective desire to respect the environment. Every home was well insulated and designed with sufficient south-side windows for passive solar heating. Neighbors shared one lawn mower and garden tools to tend the community's land, which included fruit trees and a small garden. They selected the Nomad property because retail shops, restaurants, and a major bus route were just a one-minute walk away, cutting back on the need to drive.

"Cohousing residents share a common interest to live in a neighborhood," Zev says, "where you interact with your neighbors more, have community meals together, and you

Their home in Nomad *(Courtesy of Neshama Abraham)*

take responsibility for the maintenance of the property."

The couple was excited to start their family and life together in their beautiful home and cozy community. Zev was busy professionally educating people across the country about cohousing, still in its infancy with just nineteen communities completed in the United States. (There are currently 120 in North America.) Step one in Zev's approach was to correct the perception that a cohousing community is the same as a 1970s hippie commune.

"It's the only well-known group-living model that people have heard a lot about," he explains. "So, much of the time is explaining what cohousing is, describing it as an intentional neighborhood with private home ownership with an HOA that owns a common clubhouse. I start there because that is verbiage that people understand. And then you can start to layer in that the group is self-managed, that we make decisions a form of consensus, that we do activities together like occasional shared meals and community workdays, and then it starts to fill in for people what cohousing really is."

Very quickly, Zev's work changed the course of Neshama's career. When she volunteered to help work with producers on a network television program to create a segment on cohousing, it became clear the movement needed a talented point person in PR and marketing.

"I remember speaking on the phone with one of the producers at NBC News to figure out which community they would profile, and working with the community to determine which residents wanted to be interviewed—all the things you do to make for a great story," Neshama says. "After that, everyone just said, 'Neshama, do it. Represent us.'"

Gone were the days of representing large corporations and mass-market products. Neshama became the national media contact for sustainable, environmentally responsible communities. She already had strong skills in explaining concepts, proactively working with the media, and producing material to educate people. The only challenge was how fast she needed to get up to speed on the topic.

She says, laughing, "I would say like a rocket ship!"

Neshama read all that Zev and other experts had written on the movement, and listened to him on speakerphone when he was interviewed. Within weeks, she was comfortable with tasks ranging from advising developers when they were fielding interview questions from the media to guiding group members about how to educate others about the concept. By the end of 1998, she was working daily with Zev helping to guide future residents through marketing and group dynamics programs so they could one day effectively manage environmentally conscious cohousing projects. Sustainability was now part of Neshama's vocabulary.

"One definition of 'sustainability' is to look multiple generations ahead, to determine if what you do now will have a beneficial effect if repeated over and over again and throughout generations," she explains. "The Native Americans say seven generations. Think of the seventh generation in the decision you're making now."

In February 1998, Zev and Neshama got married. Zev had signed a prenuptial agreement and was aware of the several million dollars Neshama had inherited. The money allowed them to comfortably work at home and be actively involved in raising their two daughters—Halonah, born in May 1998, and Zipporah, born the following May. The two-year check-in about whether to stay in Nomad never happened; both were happy.

"As soon as we had two children," Zev says, "and some of the neighbors began to have children as well, it just became really obvious that this was a supportive and wonderful place to be and to raise a family."

Because Neshama didn't grow up babysitting or interacting with babies, she found immense comfort in having approachable neighbors.

"There were other parents and caring adult residents around that I could go next door to and say, 'Here.'" She laughs. "I'd just hand Halonah over as a baby knowing she'd be safe. I didn't even have to say much: 'I need to take a shower.' Or, 'I need some personal time—twenty minutes.' I could get a few minutes off versus what is often the case for new parents who don't have any relief."

The ages of residents and sizes of homes in Nomad were deliberately wide ranging. Single people, empty nesters, families with children, elders, and various income levels were all represented.

"That's a piece of the social sustainability: having a diverse community," Zev explains. "It's more interesting, it's a better environment for the kids to grow up in, you've got ways of sharing information through the wisdom of age and the youthfulness of young people."

As Halonah and Zipporah grew, Zev and Neshama embraced the continued support from neighbors. So did the kids. Zipporah, now fifteen, remembers a day she fell while playing outside. She cut her leg and had the wind knocked out of her.

"I remember thinking, *Oh my gosh. My parents aren't home, I'm hurt and can't breathe*, and I was terrified," she says. "But I opened my eyes and realized, *Wait, I've got eight families around me. Which house do I want to go to?*"

Neshama felt grateful to have landed within a caring group of parents who were raising children of similar ages.

There was no need to pack up and drive to playdates; the kids would play together on the swings. They all shared hand-me-downs, cooking duties, and conversation in the common courtyard.

"I could say what I was feeling and then hear other parents' viewpoints. It was free therapy," Neshama says with a chuckle. "The kids would be playing outside and we would sit together and talk while they played. In ten minutes I felt relieved that I'd shared something that was bothering me and got really good input."

Holiday preparations were easier, too. "At Easter, we'd all meet in the common house and color eggs together. Our family created a community Passover. One year we turned the courtyard into a graveyard for Halloween."

The collective goal was to give and take. Zev recalls, "We had an older gentleman who was a neighbor of ours for quite a few years, and he sort of adopted the girls as a grandparent since our parents had passed away. He had the girls over to read stories, played with them in the courtyard, or they went together to special events like a play or musical."

Neshama developed a relationship with a young girl in the community who was living with her father after her parents' divorce. She's now sixteen.

"I've been like a mother to her. When she has

boyfriend issues she'll come over and talk with me about things," Neshama says. "We share a space in each other's lives. It's all about the longevity of the relationships and that's the cord that weaves a stable life together. When you've known people their whole lives you can count on each other."

The most challenging transition to cohousing for Neshama was the community's policy of consensus. Decisions that affected life in Nomad had to be agreed upon by a majority of residents. Before every important decision is made in the community, two meetings are held over the course of a month. It took Neshama awhile to realize that extensive conversations between neighbors ultimately result in a respectful process and a positive outcome.

"I felt impatient. I wanted things to move more quickly. I would think, *This decision makes sense. Let's just do it*. But the two-meeting time frame accommodates the person who needs to process information longer. It now makes sense to me. You learn to respect the differences in peoples' styles and become more patient," she says. "Living in community stretches you in a good way. Zev describes cohousing as 'the most extensive personal growth workshop you'll ever take. And at the end of it, you get to move into a great home in a resilient neighborhood.'"

Neshama and Zev admit the cohousing model, like

every arrangement that involves people, isn't perfect. But when problems arise, the community's experience with consensus and open communication is helpful.

"There's one neighbor who when she gets upset will sometimes yell," Neshama explains. "We had to have a conversation with her early on that shouting is not an acceptable way to speak to adults, and it's certainly not okay to yell at children because it scares them and they don't understand it. We created a community-wide agreement that if you're upset, you need to walk away. When you're calm, then it's okay to speak with the parents or kid about what happened. You can resolve things that way in a cohousing community; you can't always do that with people you don't know as well."

Eighteen years later, Nomad has grown from eighteen to thirty-one residents, ranging in age from one to seventy-four. Neshama and Zev are one of the five original households that remain; there were originally eleven.

Their daughters are now teenagers. When the girls visit friends outside Nomad, they experience the privacy of a typical suburban neighborhood. Zipporah wonders if she'll choose to live one day with her own family in the close quarters of a cohousing setup.

"I think about it a lot," she says. "I'll probably go to college and then decide whether I want to live really close to people or not."

Zipporah, Neshama, Zev, and Halonah,
Boulder, 2013 *(Courtesy of Neshama Abraham)*

Zipporah says some of her dearest friends live in Nomad and she loves her extended family there, but the layout of the community can be trying at times. The teen would slightly tweak the orientation of the homes.

"So I could go out the front door without everyone seeing me and thinking, *She's wearing a dress! Where is she going?*"

While Neshama enjoys having a steady flow of visitors to the house, she explains that neighbors can create a "Do Not Disturb" symbol that everyone in the community recognizes and honors.

"We use a pretty piece of fabric, and when it covers the glass in the top half of the door, that means 'come back later.' Other households have a different symbol," Neshama explains, "like a flag or something they display that lets people know it's not a good time to visit."

So much has changed for Neshama since her upbringing in the Columns. She's proud of the loving family she and Zev have created together.

But there is also a change she's ashamed to admit. In 2007 and 2008, the economic downturn devastated her and Zev's cohousing consulting business; virtually all of their planned projects came to a halt. Regrettably, there was no financial net. Decades of living without a budget had depleted the family's substantial bank account and savings. Neshama takes full responsibility for spending how she was raised—with no limits—and for not overseeing the managing of her money. If only she had taken the advice her wealthy cousin gave her after her mother, Amelia, died.

"I remember my cousin saying to me, 'Your one job is to keep your money. Don't worry about how much you earn, just keep and grow what you have.'"

So many emotions are tied to the fact that her mother worked so hard to earn the family fortune, and Neshama lost it.

"I have felt sad, regretful, disappointed, and sometimes envious of others who still have extra money. I want to cry when I think about it; I had no appreciation at the time for how much I had."

In the last seven years, the family's lifestyle has changed dramatically. They live on a strict budget. Halonah and Zipporah, now sixteen and fifteen, moved from private to public school. Once-lavish gifts for Hanukkah are now handmade. Neshama shops for clothes at a consignment shop.

"I have learned," she says. "You earn a dollar and you spend it thoughtfully, or you save it."

A silver lining around a very dark cloud is that Neshama is now teaching her daughters the lesson that escaped her.

"They are very aware of the value of money. When they walk into a store they know in advance what they want to buy and have discussed with us how much they have to spend. Both girls work and are responsible and budget conscious. They're growing up in a much different environment where they're developing a good sense of how to earn, save, and appropriately spend money. Plus, we've also taught them the more important value of a healthy and loving home life."

Despite the monetary loss, Neshama says she has gained infinitely more in her fifty-four years. She has nurtured a solid relationship with her daughters, transitioned to a fulfilling professional life, and loves and respects even more the man who caught her eye from across the dance floor.

"Zev changed my life much for the better. I believe I would have stayed inwardly lonely. I now feel fulfilled professionally by using my communication skills to educate people about sustainable options and to help protect the environment. I would likely have continued on my New York rat-race lifestyle, pushing myself constantly. I wouldn't have connected with nature or found the quiet within or around me. To have ended up here in community within a nurturing home and supportive neighborhood is a blessing. The richness is everybody around me."

Neshama lives just five minutes from where she sat on a swing, marveled at the Rockies, and envisioned a more meaningful life.

The universe, apparently, was listening.

What lies before us and what lies behind us are small matters compared to what lies within us. And when you bring what is within out into the world, miracles happen.

—HENRY DAVID THOREAU

# ⤖ MARGARET CHO ⤔

Comedienne Margaret Cho is a Superwoman of sorts to the people she champions: the bullied, the outliers, the eccentric. But when she was eight years old, Margaret was convinced she was Wonder Woman.

"There was no doubt in my mind. I would practice running and jumping off the steps. First one, then two, then three. When I worked up to five," she says, laughing, "I knew I was Wonder Woman and that was my journey."

It was not. By the time Margaret turned fourteen, she realized her true superpower was writing and delivering jokes. Her parents, immigrants from Korea, were encouraging but busy managing a bookstore in San Francisco.

"I think they thought I was odd, because I was. I was

an extremely focused kid with goals, like becoming a co-medienne. It's what I really wanted to do."

Margaret's high school classmates considered her odd, as well, but for different reasons. They saw a shy, awkward freshman with few friends, cloaked in the dark garb of the Goth subculture. Her knack for humor was lost on her peers.

"They might have thought I was goofy," she says, "but no one took the time to really know what kind of person I was."

A self-described "tough cookie," Margaret pushed through her feelings of isolation and focused instead on any opportunity to engage in comedy. She performed stand-up at events held at the local mall. She delivered comedy sketches in her high school drama class. Then, at age fifteen, the odd girl out in school was made to feel even more shunned. A group of girls exposed her bisexuality.

"Being queer as a kid is a big problem. You get bullied a lot in school because kids can recognize somebody who's different among them, and often the first reactions are fear and anger."

The sophomore arrived at school one day to find "Margaret Cho is a f*cking dyke" spray-painted on walls throughout the school. She was traumatized and confused. She'd not told anyone she was gay.

"These girls had fabricated instances where I kissed them. I was really insulted because I would never consider kissing them," she says with sarcasm. "Gross. Maybe her, but not you!"

In her junior year of high school, Margaret transferred to the San Francisco School of the Arts, determined to hone her comedic skills. She was eager to develop a career in comedy and move into the adult world and away from her painful youth.

"It made me very resentful and very jaded among children; I was over children and over childhood. I didn't grasp the innocence or wonder of it."

One of Margaret's teachers at the arts school recognized that her young student had a compellingly irreverent sense of humor. The woman wanted to expose Margaret to a higher level of talent, but at sixteen, she wasn't allowed in comedy clubs. Somehow, the teacher finagled a walk-on for Margaret at one of the local laugh factories.

"She signed me up for an open-mike night at a comedy club in San Francisco. I wasn't allowed to hang out in the bar and had to wait outside until I went on."

The exhilarating experience bolstered her passion for comedy. That same year, her dream found its mentor. Margaret recalls the night in 1983 when she watched comedienne Joan Rivers host *Saturday Night Live*.

"It was really profound to me. We had one of those old VCRs and I remember taping it and watching it over and over, knowing that she was the person who I idolized and that comedy was my religion."

Admitting now it wasn't a wise choice, Margaret left high school late in her junior year to pursue comedy full-time. She says her parents were busy working and weren't fully aware of her comings and goings.

"Their approach was, 'We actually have to make money so we can eat and have a house, so we'll see you later!'" she says, laughing. "They were very absent, but not in a way that was more than I could handle."

Margaret performed in as many venues as possible, lying about her age and bunking with friends. Her gut feeling that she was headed toward where she belonged was confirmed at age seventeen.

"Jerry Seinfeld saw me because I had lied my way into a college comedy competition," she explains. "The prize was to open for Jerry. When I won he said to me, 'You're so funny. You're really, really good. You should be a comedienne.' I took it and I ran with it."

Over the next twenty years, Margaret's pioneering approach to topics like sexuality, ethnicity, and nonconformity propelled her into the ranks of top-level talent and national celebrity. Her comedic range generated a prolific

Cho Dependent Tour, Atlanta, 2010 *(Courtesy of Lindsey Byrnes)*

résumé—star of television, stage, and film; author; producer; musician; Grammy and Emmy nominee; competitive dancer. She continues to serve as an activist for causes ranging from anti-bullying to pro–gay rights.

"There are things I can improve and change, and that will always be the case. But I know that I'm living on the right side of my truth, and that's a great comfort to me," she says. "I feel very lucky that I knew right away what I should be doing and that I was the kind of person who was so devoted to it and who didn't have anything in my life at that time to block my way."

But what of those roadblocks? What's the payoff for finding a way to bust through them?

"The fact is that you only have one life, and that can be taken from you at any moment. You can waste it on the desires and expectations of other people, or you can be willing to try and find out what that is for you," she says. "Often, people who don't know are just so afraid of knowing or admitting it to themselves because that would dismantle their lives entirely. People's lives grow with obligation as they grow older, and those obligations can be a mighty weight and a prison—so much so that they don't allow their mind to go where it wants to go."

Margaret Cho's mind ran straight to comedy and her heart followed, laughing all the way.

A long marriage is two people trying to

dance a duet and two solos at the same time.

—ANNE TAYLOR FLEMING

# ⤜ LINDLEY DEGARMO ⤛
# AND SARAH FINLAYSON

When Lindley DeGarmo was a boy, he wanted to become a United States senator or maybe even the president. An avid reader, Lindley enriched his daydreams with every turn of the page. He devoured biographies about George Washington, Abraham Lincoln, and John F. Kennedy. Lindley imagined how he too would one day do great things in Washington, DC. What he never dreamed was that loss would devastate him, twice, by the time he turned thirteen years old.

Lindley was born in Pine Plains, New York, a small town one hundred miles directly north of New York City. His parents, Lindley and Elsie, met at the local high school, where he worked as a math teacher, she as a nurse. Before both were thirty, the couple was raising four children: Lindley was the oldest at six, followed by his four- and two-year-old brothers, Mark and Todd, and newborn sister, Susan. The family and most of their neighbors attended one of the community's four churches. The DeGarmos worshipped at United Methodist, where the kids' Sunday school classmates were also friends from school. Lindley enjoyed learning Bible stories and singing in the children's choir.

"It never occurred to me not to believe in God when I was that age," says Lindley. "It was just sort of part of the fabric of the world at that age."

Lindley's dad had grown up on a farm in upstate New York and wanted his children to experience the fun of watching things grow, as well as the work that goes into successful gardening.

"There was always a good hour of pulling weeds," Lindley jokingly grumbles.

His father planted an extensive vegetable garden in the backyard: peas, string beans, squash, tomatoes, corn, and eggplant. Every fall, young Lindley would enter potential prizewinners in competitions at the local agricultural fair.

"I won first place from time to time," he recalls, and jokes, "I think they were generous with the ribbons."

Pine Plains was the perfect launching point to visit

relatives on both sides of the family. His mother's extended family lived two and a half hours south in Long Island, his father's two hours north in Schuylerville. Summers always meant a road trip to the DeGarmo family farm. From the time he was five, Lindley spent anywhere from two weeks to a month at the farm, playing with cousins and helping his uncle with daily chores.

"We'd go out on the hay wagons and catch bales and pile them up," he describes, "and then take the wagons back to the barn and unload the bales. My uncle had a herd of Guernsey cows and those had to be milked twice a day."

Sometimes, only Lindley and his father visited the farm. They fished for bluegills and sunfish in a meandering creek that ran beside a series of pastures, serving as both a watering hole and boundary for the dairy cows.

"I can remember a number of trips we would take. The two of us drove there before the New York State Thruway," he says, "so it was a long drive up through country roads to get there. I remember ours being a close relationship."

Tragically, in 1959, Lindley's dad was diagnosed with cancer. The cells were discovered quite late and had metastasized. A year later, he died at age thirty-one, leaving behind his wife, four small children, and no life insurance. Lindley, age seven, had abruptly lost his beloved father— and his childhood.

Lindley and his father, Schuylerville, New York, 1955 *(Courtesy of Lindley DeGarmo)*

"I think it made me more introverted than I would have been," he says. "I developed a certain chronic depression. As the oldest kid, I think early on I felt that I now had to be the man of the family, and that tended to make me a little more serious, more contemplative."

A widow with seven-, five-, three-, and one-year-olds, Elsie rejoined the workforce as a school guidance counselor. Housekeepers doubled as babysitters for the kids. Lindley says that, as a child, even with the stress of adjustment following his father's death, he never felt that a dark cloud had descended on the house; if it had, it was hovering behind a closed door.

"My mother was, and still is, a stiff-upper-lip type of person, and I think her way of coping with all that was to be strong. I don't know what her private grief was, but we never saw a lot of it," he explains. "I think the sentiment at that time was that you protect the kids from a lot of it, so for example, we didn't go to the funeral. I've spoken to my mother about that since, and we sort of agree that if we had it to do over we'd have done that part differently."

Within eighteen months, Elsie began dating Jim Smith, a business education teacher in the high school where they both worked. He was seven years her junior and had had a difficult childhood of his own. He was born to young, absentee parents and ultimately had to move in with his aunt and uncle. He also suffered from Hodgkin's lymphoma, which was in remission when he met Elsie. Now, at twenty-seven, he was dating a woman with children ranging from eight to two years old. Lindley was torn between wanting a father figure and feeling that Jim was a threat to their reestablished family.

"I had felt like the man of the family and then suddenly, obviously, I never really was," Lindley explains. "It became more obvious with a man around, and then more so when he started to want to exercise some discipline. He had been in the army and always wore a crew cut, and he was one of these guys who kept his shoes immaculately shined, so he had a side to him that was"—Lindley pauses—"'macho' is probably too strong of a word—but something like that, and so we butted heads to a certain extent."

Elsie and Jim married barely a year after they met, in November 1962, on her thirty-fourth birthday. She gave birth to a son the next year. Baby Jim made seven, and the family was on a razor-thin budget. Elsie gave the kids haircuts and made many of their clothes. Jim took a higher-paying job as a professor at a business college an hour away in Albany.

"You just didn't count on very much," says Lindley.

Along with household chores (they kept Dad's garden going), Lindley was a busy eight-year-old working on his own. He mowed lawns, gardened for neighbors, and sold vegetables in a farmers' market he and a friend set up in a rented garage. He also had a knack for door-to-door sales.

"I sent away for Christmas cards to sell. Wallace Brown was the name of the company. You could either take money, or for so many boxes sold you'd get a prize. So I worked all summer and I got myself a three-speed bike. The nice thing about living in a small town was you could easily go door to door."

The family's income stream was intermittently dammed up by Jim's illness, which would advance and then retreat. When the Hodgkin's lymphoma was so severe that Jim couldn't work, Elsie took jobs as a private-duty nurse. By 1966, four years into the marriage, Elsie was also serving as nurse to her very sick husband.

"I'm not sure I was a particularly sensitive thirteen-year-old," Lindley recalls of that year. "My stepfather hated hospitals, where he had spent so much time, and toward the end of his life, I guess he had made it clear to my mom that he would prefer to die at home. There were a few months where he was basically bedridden and she was taking care of him and administering morphine and those sorts of things. I can remember one night having to help her to move him in the bed. He was quite ill at that point, and I just couldn't wait to get done with that and leave the house and go do something with my friends. I've often looked back at that and thought, *Boy, you just were really doing everything you could to get out of there*. It was not a comfortable environment."

For Lindley, there were few places to find comfort. Mom was exhausted, loss was waiting to pounce yet again, and money was scarce.

"I remember during the last Christmas that he was alive, neighbors and people from the church came by with food and, 'Here's a little something for the kids.' It was pretty hand-to-mouth there for a while."

Jim died in March 1967. At thirteen, Lindley experienced death for the second time in seven years.

"I think I went into some sort of emotional denial for a while," Lindley says. "You go through it once, and here it is again."

What would the future hold for Lindley and how much control did he have over the journey? In the many biographies he'd read about learned men who'd made a difference in the world, attending preparatory school was a common bond among the young future leaders. Lindley spoke with his school guidance counselor and mother about leaving Pine Plains's small public school system for a more rigorous education.

In September 1967, six months after his stepfather

died, Lindley enrolled in Northfield Mount Hermon School, a private boarding school in Western Massachusetts. A scholarship paid for all but one hundred dollars of the tuition.

Elsie, too, had taken steps to better her and her family's future, based on a recommendation from her husband. Before he died, knowing his illness was fatal, Jim made Elsie promise to give book sales a try. For about a year before his death, Jim earned extra money selling World Book Encyclopedias. He knew his wife's exceptional work ethic, strong communication skills, and faith in God's plan would take her far. He was right.

"In the months after Jim died," Lindley explains, "she got going with that and she had phenomenal success. He died in March, and by that summer she won the award for top sales in the entire country."

In the fall of Lindley's freshman year at NMH, his mom embarked on a several-week tour of Europe, the prize for her sales accomplishments. Elsie continued to rise through the ranks at World Book and served as a trainer at the home office in Chicago. She lived and trained in Chicago for a year, and also flew around the country giving motivational speeches to the sales force. During that year, Lindley's younger brothers and sister lived with their grandparents in Kissimmee, Florida.

"We never became rich," Lindley says, "but the financial situation eased considerably because of that."

By then, Lindley and his brother Mark were both enrolled in NMH. World Book requested that Elsie live permanently in Chicago and work in senior management. She declined, not wanting to uproot the family yet again. They stayed in Pine Plains and Elsie commuted to Westchester County, where World Book had a branch organization. Several days during the week she stayed overnight in Yonkers; once again, housekeepers cared for Lindley's siblings.

"Family life with us," he says, "was never very ordinary."

NMH proved to be a good experience for Lindley and an effective launching pad for his academic goals. In September 1971, Lindley enrolled in Princeton University in New Jersey. He paid the tuition with financial aid, contributions by Elsie, and student loans. He also worked twenty hours per week in food services throughout college.

"I was on the hot line as a freshman, and then I got a job in the faculty club and became a bartender and catered a lot of special events. In those days I had long hair and a goatee and looked very French, so they put me in a chef's hat and I would do the flambéed desserts. Cherries jubilee," he says with a laugh. "Those were the days."

In 1974, during his junior year at Princeton, Lindley took a leave to work in Washington, DC, as a personnel clerk for the US Drug Enforcement Administration. When he returned to school, he also began coursework for a master's degree in public affairs at the Woodrow Wilson School of Public and International Affairs. During his summer break in 1976, Lindley worked as an economist intern at the US Arms Control and Disarmament Agency in DC.

By summer 1977, Lindley was ready for the real world, armed with the right degrees and some on-the-job experience. In August, he moved to New York City to work for the Exxon Corporation.

"I worked as a financial analyst in the treasurer's department, one of about a dozen mostly MBAs who were in that year's hiring class. I remember those early days as being quite exhilarating," he says. "I was young, well paid, living on my own in the greatest city in the world, with friends all around, and a challenging new professional world opened up before me."

Lindley recognized right away at Exxon that his college studies had prepared him more for economics than finance. He enrolled in night classes at the Graduate School of Business at New York University (now NYU Stern) and received an advanced professional certificate in finance in 1979.

After two years of work with Exxon in New York City, Lindley was moved to Houston, Texas, to work for one of its subsidiaries, Esso Eastern Inc., as a senior staff financial analyst. Two years later, there was yet another move. In 1982, the company relocated Lindley to Tokyo, Japan, to work as an assistant manager in Esso's finance and planning department. His next move, two years later, would allow him to put down some roots back in the States.

In June 1984, Lindley moved back to New York City to work for Salomon Brothers, a Wall Street investment bank. He was hired as a vice president in the corporate finance department. The head of the company was John Gutfreund, a take-no-prisoners leader who was dubbed in a 1985 *BusinessWeek* magazine article "the King of Wall Street." The high-stakes pressure of investment banking was both enticing and exhausting for those who chose to work in the field. Lindley discovered early on that he could calm and center himself by sharing in an hour of worship at First Presbyterian Church in Greenwich Village, just a block from his apartment.

"One of my good friends recommended the church. The liturgy and especially the preaching appealed to me," he says. "It was probing, aware of the world, intelligent. The church's music was also simply outstanding."

Work at Salomon Brothers was mentally and physically demanding and Lindley wasn't taking good care of himself. He was smoking, out of shape, and in 1986, two years into the job, he made an alarming find.

"I was traveling a lot, and during one trip I became aware that my groin was feeling odd," Lindley explains. "I had an enlarged testicle. My doctor examined me and said, 'It doesn't feel right and we need to do exploratory surgery.'"

Lindley was diagnosed with testicular cancer and a month later underwent surgery to remove the mass, which had not metastasized, as his father's cancer had.

"It was interesting because until that time I didn't realize that my father had testicular cancer. I thought he had lung cancer. It was only after I told my mother that I had testicular cancer that she said, 'Oh my God, that's what your dad had!' I wasn't freaked out for some reason," Lindley says. "It was more like, *This is a bother*." His father died at thirty-one. "When this happened I was thirty-two, so I'd already gone through the magic thirty-one. I thought more when I was thirty-one, *Oh my goodness, what's going to happen to me?* but I got through that."

Lindley continued to work during the six weeks of radiation he underwent.

"I'd work and then take a car to go get irradiated, and then walk back home from Cabrini Medical Center to my apartment on Eleventh Street," he says. "There was some impact. There was a sense of mortality. I think I got a little more serious about going to church at that point."

In 1988, Lindley experienced another unexpected sensation, but this time it was chemistry. That May, Lindley's boss, Bill, and his wife, Linda, set him up on a blind date with Sarah Finlayson. Sarah went to college with Linda and worked in the city as a vice president in institutional sales of mortgage-backed securities at Shearson Lehman Hutton. They thought Sarah and Lindley would have a lot in common. The plan was to eat dinner at Bill and Linda's house in Rye, New York. Lindley and Bill would fly in from a work trip to Bermuda to entertain clients at International Invitational Race Week, then land in Westchester County and drive twenty-five minutes to Rye for the dinner date.

But the weather had a different plan. Large storms rerouted the flight to Hartford, where Lindley and Bill had to wait to clear customs and for a car to take them to Rye, about an hour and a half away.

"We had been partying from the time we got on the boats down in Bermuda, so Bill and I rolled in two and a half hours late, and if not three sheets, then two to the wind," he recalls, laughing. "It ended up that the blind date was primarily just driving back to Manhattan with Sarah."

Enough time for Lindley to find Sarah personable, pretty, and smart.

"I remember thinking he was really quite cute with beautiful eyes," Sarah recalls. "I was thirty-five years old at that point, so I thought, *I wouldn't mind seeing him again*."

That wouldn't happen right away. Sarah was headed for a vacation in Sweden, and by the time she returned, Lindley would be on a getaway to Scotland.

In June 1988, six weeks later, the two had their first real date. Bill and Linda had good instincts. Lindley and Sarah hit it off and were engaged by Thanksgiving. The following May they were married, Sarah age thirty-six, Lindley thirty-five.

Once he was married, Lindley stopped smoking. He began training to run the 1989 New York City Marathon (which he finished) as an incentive to stay healthy. Church continued to be a source of serenity for Lindley, and he and Sarah alternated their attendance between both of their churches. She introduced Lindley to her preacher, Maurice Boyd of Fifth Avenue Presbyterian.

"He was a real artist in the pulpit. I began subscribing to his weekly sermon tapes," he explains, "and often listened to them in my car when I was on my way out of the city on the weekend."

Lindley and Sarah both had demanding jobs in the exciting but grueling high-stakes financial world. She was in the sales and trading business, where the daily high velocity

New York City, 1989 *(Courtesy of Bachrach Photography)*

on the trading floor was relentless. As an investment banker, Lindley managed expectations to constantly land the next big deal. For many in their industry, the heightened stress levels led to physical burnout and mental-health challenges.

"Anger management and substance abuse were not my issues, but I tended toward depression," Lindley explains, "which Sarah noticed after we'd been married a year or so. I was definitely having a tough time keeping myself engaged. The chairman of my company was quoted in a magazine article saying that he needed people who got up in the morning wanting 'to bite the ass off a bear.' I think I was noticing that I wasn't quite at that stage, which was an issue. I was finding it more difficult to concentrate, feeling tired, and being grumpy, particularly toward those I could afford to be grouchy with, like Sarah."

Sarah encouraged Lindley to go to therapy, something she was quite familiar with, having grown up in a trying family environment.

"I come from a background of enormous amounts of therapy," Sarah explains, "so I guess I had gotten to the point in my life at thirty-seven that it wasn't my job to work on someone else's issues. I wasn't a professional."

Lindley admits he considered therapy "a luxury for spoiled Manhattanites," but he agreed to go. He began a several-year exploration with a female psychologist who specialized in career-decision cases. She helped Lindley navigate his childhood.

"I would often find myself in tears over certain memories, and I was still trying to work out how I felt about my mother," he says. "I found so many pictures where my father was noticeably proud of me and that I was special to him. She helped me process a lot of the grief about my father and eventually sent me to a psychopharmacologist. I started getting some Zoloft originally, and I've been taking some sort of medication pretty much ever since, with good effect."

In January 1990, Lindley's hard work at Salomon Brothers was rewarded with a promotion. He was now a director with the Project Finance Group. He began work on a project to privatize the Thai telephone system. One of his favorite side benefits of the frequent international travel was exploring and analyzing his faith.

"One of my Salomon colleagues on the deal was an evangelical Christian. We spent a lot of time together in Bangkok and religion was a topic of conversation. He lived in Hong Kong and I spent a number of weekends while stopping over there going to his church with him and his family," Lindley says. "His faith was much more 'out there' than mine, and I think I was challenged to try to understand better what I believed and how it was different from what he believed. All of this got me reading—and with all that travel to Asia, there was lots of time to do it."

Despite the promotion, Lindley was feeling unfulfilled by his career path.

"I guess I had felt for a while that Salomon Brothers was not a perfect fit for me. There is a quality of competitiveness in the best investment bankers that was not my strongest suit. A lot of people say the money doesn't really matter; it's just a way of keeping score. I think for me, the game was just never that all-consuming. We were trying to put together deals that would allow our clients—and us—to make a lot of money, but there was nothing inherently worthwhile in a lot of what we were trying to achieve," he explains. "Much of the business I worked on was highly structured and negotiated. You had to live with individual transactions as they came together over months or even years. There were a lot of big egos and a constant jockeying for position and advantage. I found it hard to maintain the fevered pitch. Also, as I became a manager and began to be responsible for people's careers, I was frustrated with how hard it was to create a real team in an environment where everyone was always expendable."

Lindley resumed therapy with the same female psychologist who had helped him several years earlier.

"We talked a lot about issues I had at work, concerns I had at work. I had just been promoted, I was making a lot of money, I was getting good feedback in the form of a promotion, and yet I wasn't happy about it," he says. "So, what's going on here?"

What *was* going on? Between the two of them, the DeGarmos were making enough money to qualify as the top 1 percent of earners in the country. They lived in a spacious apartment in Brooklyn Heights.

"One of the perverse things about New York and Wall Street is, there's always someone who's doing better, and so you're less likely to say, 'How marvelous! How well I've done!' but rather you think, *I'm as good as so-and-so, why am I not doing that?* It's hard to get too uppity there."

Lindley recalls having those conflicted feelings at his sister's 1993 wedding in Pine Plains. His humble past and successful present mingled on the lawn of his mother's house. Lindley was chatting with his dad's older brother.

"We were standing out in the yard, and my car was sitting there, and I remember him looking down at it and he didn't say anything to me," Lindley describes. "I was driving the S-Class 500 Mercedes and he didn't quite know what to say. I was thinking, *This guy taught me to drive a tractor when I was twelve. What does he think?*"

The following summer brought a momentous change in the couple's life. In August 1994, at forty-one, Sarah gave birth to their daughter, Ellie. Lindley, now forty and the family's main breadwinner, took off a rare few weeks to spend with Mom and baby.

"I stayed home and we played house. Sarah had a cesarean so she was kind of out of it for a while, so I got to do a lot of the diaper changing and feeding and I just loved it," he says. "I wasn't at all prepared for how much I responded to having this little person there."

After two rewarding weeks at home, Lindley had to travel abroad for a ten-day business trip. He flew twenty-four hours to Islamabad as part of a trade delegation to discuss joint energy privatization opportunities with Pakistani officials. Trying to make a phone call to the United States—before advanced technology was available—was virtually impossible. The ten days dragged on.

"I'm thinking to myself, *I've got this baby back in New York and here I am sitting in blankety-blank Pakistan. What am I doing?*"

Within two months, they hired a weekday live-in nanny to help Sarah, who would return to work in nine months. Lindley was working full-time. Ultimately, the nanny would remain with the family for nine years.

Once Ellie was born, Lindley and Sarah both became members of the same church, the First Presbyterian Church of Brooklyn in Brooklyn Heights. The pastor, Reverend Doctor Paul Smith, had a history of fostering congregations that represented a myriad of ethnic, racial, and economic backgrounds. By the time the DeGarmos joined the church, Reverend Smith, an African American, had spent eight years creating a multiracial, multicultural, all-inclusive congregation of two hundred fifty people in the neighborhood where "Wall Street lived." Lindley was drawn to the mission and became a very active member of the church. He served as an elder and partnered with Paul in fortifying the framework for a diverse congregation.

"He was a corporate banker, so he brought organization," says Paul. "That's a very disciplined kind of organization—slide presentations, PowerPoints, five different ways to do this-that-and-the-other—and I'm just the opposite. We were a very good match because he was very well organized and I'm very spontaneous."

During the week, Lindley was finding it more and more difficult to stay engaged. His career focused on the almighty dollar, but it was instead the Almighty and religion that he found most compelling and meaningful.

"My mind was wandering increasingly away from the business things it was supposed to be focused on and toward thoughts of preaching."

Lindley turned to Paul: what would it take for him to pursue a career in the ministry?

"He started asking the more serious questions," Paul says, "like 'What do you think about this? What other kinds of courses should I concentrate on?'"

By November 1994, work provided Lindley's mind with another reason to wander.

"My dissatisfaction at Salomon was crystallized when a promotion I had been expecting did not come through," he says, "and then shortly thereafter, my immediate boss and mentor left Salomon for another firm. All this turned up the heat competitively, accentuating parts of the job that I liked least."

Could he really become an ordained minister? Should he?

Lindley kept the thoughts to himself until early 1995, when he shared with Sarah that he wanted to audit several classes in seminary.

"Sarah was not wild about the idea," says Lindley. "She worried that I was depressed or otherwise going through some sort of midlife crisis."

Sarah was blindsided. She tried to wrap her mind around the idea of Lindley trading his silk tie for a clerical collar.

"I was surprised and I didn't quite know what to think about it," Sarah explains. "I could feel there was a seismic shift in Lindley. Was it that Ellie was born? Was it not making managing director? Was it the constantly being on a plane? Something happened and he just said inside, *Enough is enough.* I could not get my arms around it. I come from a different attitude where, okay, you get knocked down and you pick yourself up and you go. So, there was a little bit of me thinking, *Why aren't you just picking yourself up and going?*"

But how do you pick up and go if you're unsure about where you're going? Lindley agreed to further examine his internal "seismic shift."

"I recognized that this was a huge and sort of nonsensical thing to be talking about, and I wasn't averse to doing things that would help decide that it wasn't crazy," Lindley says. "I agreed to see a psychiatrist and also to spend a couple of days at Johnson O'Connor Research Foundation being aptitude tested. I also opened up conversations with our pastors."

While Lindley explored, Sarah surveyed the family finances. She felt Lindley's disinterest could very well cost him his job.

"The whole next year he just sort of checked out,"

Sarah says. "He would just get on planes and go someplace. I think he went to South Africa to be a Salomon envoy or something like that. I said to him, 'Why are you going to South Africa? What's the purpose?' He said, 'I don't know.' I could just feel this pulling away. I knew he was on a downward spiral at work."

At the end of 1995, Lindley was downsized out of Salomon Brothers at age forty-two.

"Ironically, at that point I was about a year into the most intense part of my contemplation of a change. There was a part of me that felt God was giving me the push I needed to get off the dime and do it. I went ahead and enrolled as an auditor in two seminary courses that began in January, but at the same time began looking at alternatives and options for going back to work," Lindley explains. "I was pretty well-known in my field at that time, and so I took a number of calls from companies wondering if I would be interested in talking. Enron was one of these. The chief financial officer was looking to hire a head of project financing, which would have encompassed their international operations in electric power, pipelines, and so on. I would need to move to Houston again and continue the sort of global traveling that I had been doing at Salomon Brothers. I could not get interested in more of the same."

Lindley again reached out to Paul to discuss his plan to audit classes in seminary in Manhattan. Was this a man going through a midlife crisis? Paul says all signs pointed to no. Lindley had a track record of involvement with the church. He'd also shared with Paul the clarity that came into his life after having survived testicular cancer, watching a colleague yet again uproot his life for work, and having a daughter.

"As a layperson he was really involved in the church as an elder, so he knew what to expect," Paul says. "He was also looking at his friend's experience of having to move to the West Coast. He experienced losing his job. He wanted to minister. In that period of discernment, he was carefully looking at *What do I want to do? What will Sarah think about this?*"

Sarah was in shock.

"This was really quite scary. I was thinking, *This is really odd. I didn't marry a minister.* I didn't grow up in a religious or faith-based home. I grew up Presbyterian, but we were the quintessential Christmas-and-Easter people, if that. It was bizarre." She thought, *Lindley? Called to the ministry?* "The joke was, 'Whoever's calling you, Lindley, have them call me because I want to talk to them.' We lived a very expensive lifestyle and he was talking about basically making no money. He said, 'Some ministers make twenty-five to thirty thousand dollars a year.' And I knew that wouldn't even pay for the nanny. That wouldn't pay for Ellie's school. So, I sort of put that away somewhere and thought, *This is not really real.*"

Any communication issues the DeGarmos had before in their marriage were magnified by having to address Lindley's potential extreme career change. They decided to enter couple's counseling.

"I felt we were on a slippery slope," Sarah says, "meaning that if I gave an inch, Lindley would take a foot or two feet. I knew that if he started auditing and he liked it, the next shoe was going to drop."

They carved out time once a week for counseling.

"She gets angry and I withdraw," Lindley says. "I shut down. So, I'm not going to say I was angry because that's not how it manifested. But I certainly was frustrated."

Why was it wrong for him to consider a new and more meaningful direction in life? Generations that came before Lindley valued work that advanced general welfare, not personal fulfillment. But Lindley was born in 1953.

"There's a tension there, isn't there?" Lindley says. "Notions of duty and self-sacrifice predominated at one time. But we baby boomers have been more inclined to privilege self-realization over the old values. At what point does pursuing your own happiness regardless of the cost to others become just plain selfish? I think at the time I was probably more self-righteous than feeling selfish or guilty." He adds, "Those emotions came later, I am embarrassed to say."

The DeGarmos also sought the counsel of close friends and their pastor, Paul. He says Sarah reminded him of his own wife, Fran.

"Fran's her own person. She doesn't think of herself as a pastor's wife. She's a schoolteacher, so she makes it very clear that *I* was called," Paul says, chuckling, "not her."

In January 1996, Lindley began to audit several classes at Union Theological Seminary. He deliberately sampled the new direction part-time, knowing that his wary wife could be the roadblock to the path's becoming permanent. Sarah was nervous about the family's economic outlook. Lindley's earning potential was unclear, and there was growing instability at her company, where a merger was under way. She did her best to stay strong and positive.

"If the tables were turned," Sarah explains, "and this was a man looking at his wife, say, going from finance to becoming an artist, the world would just say, 'A man's gotta do what he's gotta do,' right? So, I believed it was the right thing. I also thought historically, *C'mon. My father was a POW in Germany. This is nothing.* We were healthy, we had food on the table, we had a beautiful daughter, and I had a left-turn husband. I could deal with it."

Sarah's supportive approach was admirable but also rooted in sheer exhaustion.

"I didn't have the energy. There were too many other things going on. We were dealing with a one-year-old baby, my father had just died, my husband lost his job and was not sure where he was going, and then I had my mother in Florida who had early-onset Alzheimer's and we were trying to figure out where to put her. There was a lot of stuff going on in addition to Lindley's change. My job at that point was to keep my head down and make sure all our bills were paid."

Lindley felt more secure about their short-term financial future. When he left Salomon Brothers, he took with him deferred income that was realized over about five years. He felt the time was now to investigate the option of a new career path.

"I think for one thing I was incredibly stubborn—something Sarah and other friends remarked on at the time," Lindley admits. "And I do think there's an element of ego and selfishness in that: *I know what's best even though logic says otherwise and you disagree with me.* I was also feeling very justified by the way my initial foray into auditing seminary courses was going and how I was filling my hours at home. It all felt right. Sarah liked my being at home more often even though she was rooting for me to find a job. Ellie was young and I really liked being there to watch her grow."

In September 1996, Lindley enrolled full-time in Union Theological Seminary. He felt confident he was making the right decision and that he and Sarah were committed to working things out as a couple through counseling.

Lindley's dream was to attend seminary at Princeton Theological Seminary, but he knew Sarah would not be on board with yet another compromise: a move to New Jersey.

"By and large, my good friends and family were pretty supportive. Acquaintances and colleagues were more frequently polite and somewhat puzzled. There were a few friends who were vocally concerned for my sanity," Lindley says. "Several advised Sarah to get a divorce."

Sarah continued her work in finance, Lindley in seminary. He admits life was somewhat lonely.

"It was sometimes," Lindley says. "I was spinning off in this whole world of seminary and she didn't really share in that. Part of that was that I was off doing classwork during the day, which was like my job, and she had her job and it was demanding. There was no, 'Hey, what happened today?' The quality of the relationship was strained there for a while, no doubt. We just had less time together that was fun and unforced. We never stopped being friends through all of this, but for a few years it was kind of tough."

For Sarah, life was a blur.

"I would leave our apartment at five fifteen in the morning and I would go to work," she says. "I would leave between five thirty and six and get home hopefully by six thirty or seven and then do it all over again."

Lindley thrived in seminary. He loved the coursework, the broad range of subject matter.

"There's language, there's literature, history, and I'd long had an interest in the Bible but, like most people, wasn't familiar with it. So I got immersed in that with some terrific teachers who really brought it alive." For Lindley and the other seminary students, academics provided the necessary support to discuss faith in a meaningful way. "It's not like you're going into a cloistered life and becoming more experientially linked to God somehow. It's trying to absorb the tradition and the intellectual part of it so you have something to talk about as you go out and practice the profession down the road."

Lindley's colleagues at seminary became his new set of "work" friends. In his second and third years of study, Lindley interned in churches—including Paul's—which led to professional relationships.

"You begin to have parishioners respond to you," Lindley explains, "so gradually you build a new world of support and interaction."

Lindley had made the transition to the seminary, but Sarah says his spending habits did not. From the start of their relationship, Lindley was always the spender, Sarah the saver. She says initially, they helped each other come more to the middle. But once their hefty annual income disappeared, Sarah implemented some lifestyle changes. They traded in their Mercedes for a more affordable car. Annual donations of $50,000 to charity were decreased significantly. Plans in place to help Lindley's family members were halted.

"We always had our own rental house in the Hamptons, and then suddenly we were guests of people. My sense of financial security was changed big-time," she says. "If Lindley had kept working we would have been a whole lot better off and that would have enabled more freedom for me on some level. I'm not a materialist; I don't care about things. I'd rather have more money in the bank and security. That's always been my thing. It just all became more precarious. Where I'd thought we were headed was not where we were headed."

Money was a heated topic during couple's counseling.

"Lindley wanted a spiritual life *and* a nice lifestyle. I resented that he wanted me to pony up and give him that lifestyle. I curbed his spending, but for instance, while he was in seminary he had a personal trainer, and I said, 'What are you doing? You have a trainer who costs seventy-five hundred dollars a year.' I think he didn't understand why I was so angry. He didn't understand the sacrifices that I was making. He didn't get it."

Lindley acknowledges that on some level he was stubborn about curbing his spending habits, but that perhaps some of Sarah's aggravation was actually directed at his pursuing a more fulfilling profession.

"I always maintained that if Sarah was unhappy with her career, she had the same option as I: to do something different. If that meant further adjustments to our lifestyle, we would make them."

Serendipitously, in the late 1990s, Sarah's industry boomed.

"My job took off and my income growth covered much of what Lindley wasn't bringing in. So, the money came," Sarah says. "It would have been entirely different, I think, if my career had failed. That would have been even more difficult."

Beyond finances, Sarah says the supportive role she played in Lindley's career transition was often overshadowed by a certain "halo effect" created by people's perception of the ministerial field. After all, who was she to question her husband's calling?

"Of all the professions he could choose, this is a

profession that people are in awe of, and I would get comments like, 'What a journey's he's on!' or 'Isn't it amazing what he's doing? Can you imagine leaving banking and becoming a minister?' There was one woman who I met and she said, 'I'll bet no one ever asks you, "How's your journey?"' And I said, 'You know, you're right.'"

Sarah and Lindley continued to talk through their challenges in counseling, the impact of their own past personal losses and their issues as a couple. Neither had imagined the blueprints for their future would need to be redrawn.

"There were a few moments where I thought, *This isn't gonna make it*," Lindley says. "There were one or two times that she would become so frustrated and angry that I thought, *Unless I'm willing to fold, which I don't see how I can, I don't know how we're ever going to reconcile*. I was devastated—*Oh my goodness, the bottom is dropping out*—a much more desperate feeling than I had with my cancer diagnosis. I think the desperation came from the fact that I didn't feel like I would be true to myself not to do what I was doing."

Sarah says she could not face the idea of a divorce on top of all the other challenges brewing in their life.

"We were sitting on the bed at one point and Lindley said to me, 'I thought we would always make it together.'

It was a pivotal point. I thought, *I can't throw the baby out with the bathwater. I've got to make this work.* I liked him. I liked having him in my life, so there must have been that overwhelming pull for me, but it took awhile."

As their pastoral counselor, Paul saw that the way for them to stay together was clear but difficult to execute.

"How could Lindley be Lindley," Paul says, "without making it difficult for Sarah to be Sarah?"

In May 1999, Lindley was awarded a master of divinity degree at forty-five years old. The following February, he was ordained as a Presbyterian minister of the Word and Sacrament.

"The day I was ordained was an incredible high," Lindley says, "right up there with my wedding day in terms of feeling loved and blessed and supported."

The next step was the first step in Lindley's new career as a full-fledged minister. He was eager to find a call and become the senior person at a church. Lindley knew Sarah didn't want to move out of New York, so he found an opening on the west side of the Hudson that would allow her to easily commute into Manhattan for work. Sarah did not give it her blessing. He agreed to take a lesser position as interim associate pastor at his former church, First Presbyterian in Greenwich Village.

Lindley, Ellie, and Sarah, First Presbyterian Church,
New York City, 2000 *(Courtesy of Lindley DeGarmo)*

"There were a couple of fundamental things that I felt I had to give up," he says, "but the bigger give has been from Sarah."

In March 2000, a little more than four years after the pink slip from Salomon Brothers, Lindley started his new job as an interim pastor at First Presbyterian. He was now looking out over the pews instead of sitting in one. Sarah and Lindley had arrived at a place where they wanted more than just to stay married; they wanted a gratifying relationship.

"I think that was the work that was paramount for us to do," Sarah says. "That was the work we did with the therapist weekly for two years. After those two years I just said to myself, *This is who he is, this is where we're going, and we have a little girl who's growing up and I love her and he loves her*, and he got a job and it was a good job."

In Greenwich Village, after eighteen years in the same career, Lindley began the transition into a field far removed from corporate finance and Wall Street.

"The professional church world has its own language and rituals. A lot of it was new to me when I started. Now I am reasonably comfortable among my peers, although I am a bit of an odd duck, having come to it so late and from such a different world," says Lindley. "Certainly, 'church speak' was not the norm in the investment banking world."

Two and a half years into Lindley's job as an interim associate pastor, a fork in the road presented itself—a fork that headed south to Maryland. Lindley was being considered for a position as pastor and head of staff at a six-hundred-fifty-member Presbyterian church in Towson, a suburb of Baltimore. This was his chance to lead a church. Lindley and Sarah visited the area in November 2002, and one month later, several members of the pastoral nominating committee traveled to New York City to formally extend an offer to Lindley.

"It was acknowledged at that point that a big part of our decision would revolve around Sarah's feelings and career opportunities," says Lindley. "I agreed to give them an answer by late January."

During the Christmas holiday, Lindley and Sarah drove back to Baltimore to tour Towson and the surrounding area. Unfortunately, Sarah developed a stomach virus and missed most of the outings. When the deadline came for Lindley to reply to the offer, Sarah was not yet convinced the move was a good option. Lindley respectfully declined.

"I didn't really want to uproot the family," Sarah says, "and I would say to Lindley, 'Why can't you get something in New York?' It took me awhile to get my arms around leaving New York."

Lindley was disappointed.

"I thought it was a pretty good fit for us. But I was also clear that if Sarah didn't agree wholeheartedly, it was never going to work," Lindley says. "I was also trying to let her know that I respected her decision and remained confident that we'd eventually find something that clicked for all of us."

Sarah spent several weeks revisiting the pros and cons of making a major move. The Towson job would not pay Lindley what he made ministering in New York, but the family's quality of life would improve handsomely. The risk of terror attacks would decrease; the amount of green space would increase. Money would go further. Lindley would have a chance to run his own church. Having just turned fifty, Sarah began to warm up to the idea of leaving behind decades of taxing commutes and long workdays. She wanted to spend more time with eight-year-old Ellie.

"I had no life in New York City. The joke for me was that I didn't live in Brooklyn, I slept in Brooklyn," Sarah says.

The last piece in Sarah's decision-making process fell into place when she asked her employer if they would set up an office for her in Baltimore. When they agreed, Sarah was on board with a move. The Towson job had remained available, and the position was reoffered to Lindley.

In 2003, the DeGarmos were off in a new direction—this time, as a unified force. In October, ten months after the initial offer, Lindley was installed as the ninth pastor of Towson Presbyterian Church.

"The church was packed with friends old and new. There were words of encouragement and faith in the future. I never got that kind of feedback on Wall Street," says Lindley. "A bonus check just isn't the same quality of love."

Paul, whom Lindley calls his mentor, was there to support his close friend and colleague.

"I think the congregation learned something really valuable both about Lindley and Sarah because of the struggle in making the decision," Paul says. "Sarah is a very strong person, and she made it very clear that she had done well with her career and she was moving in a direction that she wanted to go, but at the same time she loved Lindley and Lindley loved her. They had some very good time of discernment through prayer, through faith, through disagreement, and yet, through it all they were able to balance what Lindley needed, what Sarah needed, and what community Ellie would grow up in. I think they are a stronger, loving couple because they went through this experience together."

The move to Towson proved to be a positive one for the whole family.

"It has certainly made me more physically available," Lindley says. "I've made it my practice in Towson to always get home for dinner, even if I have to return to the church in the evening for meetings. That was just not an option in the Salomon Brothers days. I would also like to think that I am a calmer, more sensitive presence to those I love because of my own spiritual maturation during these years. Then too, for Sarah and me, the process of working through the change was one of mutual discovery and growth. Hopefully, I've become a little less self-involved in it all. I've come to realize this isn't just about me doing what's right for me; it's about the change we've all made. In some ways I've been stubborn and led us in this direction and it's been tough, especially for Sarah. With twenty/twenty hindsight I can say the change was a good one for me and—as it turned out—my family. We have been blessed."

The transition for Sarah took several years. Lindley had a congregation and Ellie had schoolmates, but Sarah was without colleagues for the first time in her life. She made it a point to forge relationships by becoming involved with youth sports, coaching, and being a team manager.

"I think it's been a great change," says Sarah. "Ellie has blossomed down here. She's become quite a gifted lacrosse player, which we would never have found out unless we got her out of New York. It's an easier way of life; Lindley has grown into his job, and I had a good eight years with my job."

In June 2007, Lindley's mom, Elsie, moved to Towson. She never remarried after being widowed twice.

"We kid with my mom that she gave up on men after that," Lindley chuckles. "She was just too deadly."

Elsie, Sarah, and Ellie are all members of the church Lindley heads. Dad presided when Ellie was confirmed by the church at age thirteen.

"She's like most of the kids who are confirmed," says Lindley. "We don't see as much of them once they're confirmed. We've never taken a very hard hand in saying to Ellie, 'You've got to go.' Sarah's there just about every week. She's become my chief editor. She reads my sermon ahead of time, and she's a pretty tough critic."

So what is it like for Lindley to be a minister? He says there are many lovely components to his job, but like all careers, work is work. Being a pastor has its own set of pressures and challenges.

"I think the toughest part of heading a church for someone like me—who understands numbers—is dealing with the sort of secular decline of the mainstream church that is under way. There are fewer Presbyterians every year, for example, and they attend church less frequently than they used to. That means it's harder to fill pews and there

Sarah, Lindley, and Ellie, Ireland, 2014 *(Courtesy of Sarah Finlayson)*

is an ongoing pressure on budgets," he explains. "When I started out, I envisioned myself as being so effective as a preacher and pastor that I would, through force of my own abilities, overcome those trends in my congregation. I've become more humble, but I still feel the pressure of numbers."

Lindley says there are certainly days that feel more trying than spiritual.

But, oh, the rewarding days; the chance to share in life's most intimate and meaningful moments.

"Ministering through 9/11 and its aftermath at First Presbyterian in New York City was a uniquely rewarding time to be a pastor. We were in the thick of it and lost seven members. From opening the church that first day and conducting services every night for a week, to grieving with the families who had lost loved ones and conducting their funeral services, I felt very involved and useful."

Lindley considers baptisms among his favorite honors.

"I like to hold the baby after the formal part is done and to walk around the sanctuary introducing the little one to his or her 'brothers and sisters in Christ.' I've now been at it long enough to see some of the kids I've baptized growing into young adults in the church and I've always been their pastor."

He recalls a particularly poignant wedding.

"I married one eighty-nine-year-old and his seventy-five-year-old bride in his living room; he couldn't be too far from his oxygen. They were like teenagers with each other, so very happy."

Lindley says his early relationship with death has been very helpful in ministry. Not being included in his father's funeral has shaped his input during pastoral sessions.

"When I counsel parents now in a similar situation I always say, 'The best thing you can do is have the kids be a part of it. Let them grieve and let them see you grieve.' You're never too heavy-handed about this type of thing, but my advice, only when it is sought or when it is appropriate to offer, is, 'This is all part of the process. Don't be afraid of it.'"

In May 2008, Lindley was awarded a doctor of ministry degree by Princeton Theological Seminary. When asked to look back over the last nineteen years and the risks he took for happiness, Lindley offers, "I must admit, I tend to think of this in religious terms. Christians believe God is always calling us into relationship with God. He gives each of us gifts to be used for the common good. We all (not just preachers) have vocations, a word that comes from the Latin *vocare*, meaning 'to call.'"

Lindley then shares a beautiful phrase from Frederick Buechner, a popular writer who is also a Presbyterian minister.

"He once defined vocation as 'the place where our deep gladness meets the world's deep need.' So getting your life right has a lot to do with discerning your vocation and living it out."

*The place where our deep gladness meets the world's deep need.*

And if you're the DeGarmos, it's the place where the ones you love are standing right next to you.

## ⤜ CONCLUSION ⤛

We've all met someone who's seemingly operating on all cylinders: happy at work, great home life, active in the community, full of faith. Somehow, they've "arrived." Meantime, we're secretly second-guessing ourselves and the choices we've made in shaping our journey. I don't like feeling doubt and I'll bet you don't either.

Clearly, we all want to feel definitively that we're where we belong in life—that we're among like minds, following our dreams, serving others, imparting hope. But if we haven't yet landed in that sweet spot, how do we find it? As you've discovered in each of the previous chapters, there's clearly no single—or simple—"how-to" strategy.

Michelle knew where she belonged, but because of her

upbringing, she meandered for several years. Still, she ultimately listened to the voice in her heart and was willing to risk failure to pursue a fulfilling career path. The bigger fear for Michelle was regret.

Decades passed before Craig and Kathi embraced a change. When they did—with a leap of faith—it rewarded them in ways a generous bank account never could. Their life looks nothing like it once did. It's not supposed to.

Neshama was lonely as a child, driven as an adult. When love led her from the city to the mountains, belonging opened its doors and welcomed her inside. A community of like-minded people healed old wounds and redefined for her what it means to be a family.

A yearning to belong nearly cost Lindley and Sarah their marriage. He had a calling—not from God, but from within himself. The "team" was tested by his decision, but it was ultimately Sarah's faith in her love for Lindley that kept them together. They are a stronger couple for the struggle.

The payoff for all the people in this book—including our celebrities—is a rich story to tell, one that inspires and offers hope to any of us who wonder if we too can identify where we belong and take the first step in that direction. Their stories remind us that the very thing we're afraid of may instead be the thing that sets us free. Or that when we feel like tucking tail and running back to our old life, regret may be waiting on the doorstep. And that perhaps, *I can't possibly get there from here* is flawed thinking.

Why not, in our busy lives, sit back for a moment, reflect honestly, and ask, *Am I where I belong?* Ideally, you are.

But, if you could feel happier, more centered, grateful, relieved, and excited to live each day . . . would you make a change?

~~Should.~~

~~Would.~~

~~Could.~~

Did.

# ✈ ACKNOWLEDGMENTS ✦

My heartfelt thanks:

To Jon Karp, who once again shared a brilliant concept for a book. The guy not only knows what will strike a chord within us all, he hopes the connection will inspire us to live our best lives.

To Marysue and her artful editing. She asks the right questions, the ones that make each story richer and the entire book better. Plus, she's lovely and fun.

To the incredibly special people in this book who will change lives having told us about theirs. Life stories can be messy, and these brave folks generously offered the honest and sometimes uncomfortable details of their journeys. And the happy endings? They didn't just happen—everyone in these pages did the work.

And finally, to my dear friend Jane Lorenzini . . . wow . . . number three! Hard to believe, huh, Janie? You are a brilliant writer who somehow makes it look so easy. It's as if when you exhale poetry comes out. I am forever amazed, and am blessed and honored to have you in my life.

# ➤➤ ABOUT THE AUTHORS ◀◀

HODA KOTB has cohosted the fourth hour of *Today* since 2008. She joined NBC in 1998 as a correspondent for *Dateline*. A *New York Times* bestselling author, Kotb has written two prior books, *Hoda: How I Survived War Zones, Bad Hair, Cancer, and Kathie Lee* and *Ten Years Later: Six People Who Faced Adversity and Transformed Their Lives*. In 2015, Kotb was honored with a Gracie Award for Outstanding Host in News/Non-Fiction and a Webby Award for her "Truly Brave" music video, shining a light on pediatric cancer. The three-time Emmy winner also received Gracie Awards in 2003 and 2008, an Alfred I. duPont–Columbia University Award in 2008, a Peabody Award in 2006, and an Edward R. Murrow Award in 2002. She resides in New York City.

JANE LORENZINI has been a professional writer for three decades, including a fifteen-year career as a television news anchor and reporter. She is a two-time *New York Times* bestselling author. In 2010, she cowrote Hoda Kotb's auto-biography, *Hoda: How I Survived War Zones, Bad Hair, Cancer, and Kathie Lee*. In 2013, Jane and Hoda cowrote *Ten Years Later*, a compilation of six inspirational life stories. This book represents Jane and Hoda's third collaboration. Jane lives in Tennessee.